Human Nature: Fact and Fiction

Also available from Continuum:

What Philosophy Is, edited by Havi Carel and David Gamez

What Philosophers Think, edited by Julian Baggini and Jeremy Stangroom

Human Nature: Fact and Fiction

Edited by Robin Headlam Wells and Johnjoe McFadden

continuum

Continuum International Publishing Group
The Tower Building
11 York Road
London SE1 7NX

80 Maiden Lane
Suite 704
New York 10038

British Library Cataloguing-in-Publication Data
A catalogue record for this book is available from the British Library.

ISBN: HB: 0-8264-8545-6
PB: 0-8264-8546-4

Library of Congress Cataloging-in-Publication Data

Human nature: fact and fiction / edited by Robin Headlam Wells, Johnjoe McFadden.
   p. cm.
  Includes index.
  ISBN: 0-8264-8545-6 (hardcover) – ISBN 0-8264-8546-4 (pbk.)
  1. Act (Philosophy) 2. Human behavior – Philosophy. 3. Psychology – Philosophy.
I. Wells, Robin Headlam. II. McFadden, Johnjoe.
  B105.A35H86 2006
  128′.4–dc22

2005022985

Typeset by Servis Filmsetting Ltd, Manchester
Printed and bound in Great Britain by MPG Books Ltd, Cornwall

Contents

Contributors

Simon Baron-Cohen is Professor of Developmental Psychopathology at the University of Cambridge and Fellow at Trinity College, Cambridge. He is Director of the Autism Research Centre (ARC) (www.autismresearchcentre.com). He has been awarded prizes from the American Psychological Association, the British Association, and the British Psychological Society for his research into autism. He is author of *Mindblindness* (1995), and *The Essential Difference: Men, Women and the Extreme Male Brain* (2003).

Catherine Belsey is Distinguished Research Professor of Critical and Cultural Theory at Cardiff University. In *Critical Practice* (1980, 2002) she explained the new theories of language and culture which have changed the shape of the humanities. Her other books include *Desire: Love Stories in Western Culture* (1994), *The Subject of Tragedy* (1985) and *Shakespeare and the Loss of Eden* (1999). *Poststructuralism: A Very Short Introduction* (2002) does exactly what it says on the cover, and her *Culture and the Real* (2005) argues that human beings live precariously at the interface between the organic world and culture.

Joseph Carroll has published books on Matthew Arnold and Wallace Stevens. In *Evolution and Literary Theory* (1995), he integrated traditional concepts of literary meaning with Darwinian views of human nature and used this framework to criticize poststructuralist theory. In subsequent essays, he has continued to develop the theory and methods of Darwinian literary study. Some of these essays have been collected in *Literary Darwinism: Evolution, Human Nature, and Literature* (2004), and he has also produced an edition of Darwin's *Origin of Species* (2003). He is currently working on a Darwinian critique of Victorian novels.

Rita Carter is a science writer specializing in human brain function. Her books include *Mapping the Mind* (1998) *Consciousness* (2002) and – in the series 'Use Your Brain', of which she is editor – *Memory* (2005). The first was shortlisted for the Rhone Poulenc science prize and has been translated into 12 languages. She is currently working on a book about the nature of the self.

Gabriel Dover was a lecturer in the Department of Genetics and Fellow of King's College, Cambridge and Professor of Genetics at the University of Leicester. Currently, he is a Leverhulme Trust Research Fellow, and lives in Oxford. In his book *Dear Mr Darwin: Letters on the Evolution of Life and Human Nature* (2000), and in his book in progress, *Nurture! Nurture! Nurture!*, he emphasizes that there is a subjective 'singularity' at the heart of each individual's human nature that is not reducible to biological or cultural universals.

A. C. Grayling is Professor of Philosophy at Birkbeck College, University of London. He is the author of many books, and a frequent contributor to newspapers, radio and television. He is a Contributing Editor of *Prospect* magazine, and a Fellow of the World Economic Forum.

Ania Loomba is Catherine Bryson Professor of English at the University of Pennsylvania. She is the author of *Gender, Race, Renaissance Drama* (1989), *Colonialism/Postcolonialism* (1998) and *Shakespeare, Race and Colonialism* (2002), and numerous articles on Renaissance literature, colonial history and culture, and contemporary India. She is co-editor of *Postcolonial Shakespeares* (1998), and *Postcolonial Studies and Beyond* (2005). She is currently co-editing a documentary companion to the study of race in early modern

England, and also working on a book on contact between Renaissance England and the East.

Kenan Malik is a writer, lecturer and broadcaster. His academic interests include the history of ideas, the history and philosophy of science, and theories of human nature. He trained as a neurobiologist and was a research psychologist at Sussex University's Centre for Research into Perception and Cognition. His books include *The Meaning of Race* (1996) and *Man, Beast and Zombie* (2000) which the late Roy Porter described as 'the most thoughtful and insightful assessment of the contemporary claims of science'. He has made a number of TV documentaries and is a regular presenter of *Analysis* on Radio 4. An archive of his work can be found at www.kenanmalik.com.

Ian McEwan was born in 1948 and lives in London. His recent novels are *Enduring Love, Amsterdam, Atonement* and *Saturday.*

Johnjoe McFadden is Professor of Molecular Genetics at the University of Surrey where his research is focused on developing new approaches to tackling infectious diseases. He is author of *Quantum Evolution* (2000) and writes articles for national newspapers on topics ranging from the safety of GM food to the evolution of altruism to quantum mechanics.

Steven Pinker is Johnstone Family Professor of Psychology at Harvard University. He is the holder of four honorary doctorates, and has received numerous awards for his teaching, his research on language and mind, and his critically acclaimed popular science books *The Language Instinct* (1994), *How the Mind Works* (1997), and *The Blank Slate* (2002); the latter two were finalists for the Pulitzer Prize in Non-fiction.

Philip Pullman has published nearly twenty books, the most famous of which is the trilogy *His Dark Materials.* He has been honoured with many prizes, including the Carnegie Medal, the *Guardian*

Children's Book Award, the Whitbread Book of the Year Award – the first time in the history of that prize that it was given to a children's book – and the Eleanor Farjeon Award for children's literature. Nicholas Hytner's stage adaptation of *His Dark Materials* at the National Theatre has been described by Andrew Marr as 'a great new British myth . . . here is a story that will endure for generations'.

Robin Headlam Wells is Professor of English and Director of the Centre for Research in Renaissance Studies at Roehampton University. His most recent books are *Shakespeare on Masculinity* (2000), *Neo-Historicism* (2000) and *Shakespeare's Humanism* (2005).

Foreword

Readers of the admonition over the gates at Delphi to 'know thyself' have standardly assumed that the advice is something for individuals to take individually. According to some theories of human nature, the advice can indeed only be followed individualistically, on the grounds that there is no such general thing as 'human nature'. But with very few and usually eccentric exceptions, every ethical outlook premises the idea that there is a best thing human beings can be, consistent either with their nature or at least some optimizable part of it. And that means that almost every ethical outlook rests on an explicit or implicit theory about traits, characteristics, fundamental endowments and natural constraints shared by the featherless bipeds (this being Aristotle's zoological definition of humankind) who dominate the planet.

So, for one important example, the codifications of 'human rights' which the international community adopted after the Second World War rested on quite general beliefs about what is required as the minimum framework for human flourishing: the protection of life, of liberty, of choice in matters of personal relationships and beliefs, of privacy, of fair access to social goods and opportunities, and the like. These in turn were derived from simple observations about the kinds of things that members of our highly intelligent and social species must at least have in order to have a chance of thriving: safety, relationships, and the freedom to satisfy their basic needs and to exercise their talents in the pursuit of satisfaction.

At the uncomplicated level of these thoughts – they are the sort at which international committees arrive when trying to appease different ethnic, cultural and political constituencies – the idea that there is nothing general that can be said about human nature, and therefore minimum human needs, would seem (so a critic might say) just the sort of nonsense that salaried professors of philosophy produce in their self-regarding efforts to be controversial. And the point has a certain force. For when in 1946 Eleanor Roosevelt convened the highly international committee that drafted the United Nations Declaration of Human Rights – welcomed by all Third World countries at the time, opposed by the great powers concerned to keep a free hand in their colonies – empirical evidence about what conduces to human well-being and (more to the point) suffering was everywhere about them in the devastations of Europe and the Far East: the ruined cities, the frightful prison camps, the graveyards and wreckage of peoples and civilizations. Had a thinker in the comfort of his study announced that the UN Declaration was pointless because there is no single thing that any two human beings could be said, by way of generalization about their shared humanity, to be and therefore to need in common, he would have been laughed to scorn.

But the ground that such a thinker gives – that the idea of shared humanity is a false abstraction – should not be dismissed too quickly. It focuses attention on the fact that culture and circumstance have a huge effect on the creation of human differences. The argument is sometimes accordingly advanced that there is in fact a radical incommensurability between individuals embedded in different such settings; think of the contrast between, say, a native of the Amazon rain forest and a software engineer in Paris, both living and flourishing in their respective environments today. What they have in common, it might be said, is what either of them has in common with a zebra; and their divergences are as correspondingly large.

But it is possible to argue that the two broad claims implicit in the foregoing – that there is such a thing as human nature, on which talk of human rights and allied moral discourses depend, and that there are immense differences between individuals and peoples considered as socially constructed entities – are in fact consistent. For they address humankind under different descriptions: as natural, and as historical. Of course the former constrains the latter – historical man cannot jump fifty feet into the air unaided by one or other of the machines he has invented – and the latter shapes (distorts, enhances, extends, redirects) the former in ways that would be scarcely recognizable to a remote ancestor. (What would an Australopithecine make of a stockbroker in a taxi, wearing a pinstripe suit and self-winding watch?)

This suggestion invites an examination of the difference between human (animal) nature and human (social) nature and the possible one–many relationship that connects the former to the latter. Is this the right way to address the problem? At the very least it prompts us to be alert to the series of questions one might ask of monolithically inclined sociobiologists, relativistically inclined postmodernists, and all theoretical points between, about the level of explanation they offer (say: reductively biological as opposed to holistically ideological), and the degree to which they admit the influence of feedback between the innate and the acquired in the formation of human identities both individual and collective.

If it were right to see matters in these terms, it would be right also to avoid the temptation to take too quickly either the innate or the acquired as fundamental. This is what competing theories of human nature frequently do, forgetting perhaps that human beings might innately be socially self-creating in precisely the way that makes them seem not to have a shared nature. Such a view would amount to an inextricability thesis, as one might call it; the inextricability of the natural and cultural factors prompting us to refocus the debate on to an arguably more vital matter: the role of art and literature in enhancing what, appropriately, was once called humankind's 'higher nature', for that is where much that is best about human possibility resides.

The essays in this volume address exactly this divide – or bridge? – between biology and culture in pursuit of answers to the elusive questions posed by the very idea, whether empty or not, of 'human nature'. The debate is by far one of the most important we (as a species) can have with ourselves, for the answers to it underwrite much that matters most crucially to our well-being and our hopes, and some- times – when great conflicts come – to our very existence.

Acknowledgements

In May 2004 an international group of distinguished writers, scientists and literary theorists met at the Institute of Contemporary Arts in London to debate one of the most controversial topics of our time – the problem of human nature. The papers in this volume are based on the talks given at the symposium.

The symposium was jointly hosted and sponsored by the Federal University of Surrey (now the University of Surrey and Roehampton University) and the ICA in association with the University of Missouri-St Louis. *The Times* Newspaper co-sponsored the event. We are particularly grateful to the following for their encouragement and support: Bernadette Porter (formerly Rector, University of Surrey Roehampton), Patrick Dowling (Vice Chancellor, University of Surrey), John Turner (Deputy Vice Chancellor, University of Surrey), Mike Watts (formerly Federal Professor, University of Surrey Roehampton), Michael Kipps (formerly Federal Professor, University of Surrey), Philip Dodd (Director, ICA), Rachel Cottam (formerly Director of Talks, ICA), Mark Burkholder (Dean of Arts and Sciences, University of Missouri-St Louis), Barbara Kachur (Chair of English, University of Missouri-St Louis), Hilly Janes (Editor, *Body & Soul, The Times*) and Alison Denyer (formerly External Relations Officer, Roehampton University). Neil Taylor, Liam Gearon and Kevin McCarron all gave helpful advice.

We are also grateful to Claire Fox (The Institute of Ideas), A. C. Grayling (Birkbeck College, University of London), Michael Gove (*The Times*) and Mark Henderson (*The Times*) who all chaired sessions at the symposium.

Robin Headlam Wells, Roehampton University
Johnjoe McFadden, University of Surrey

Introduction

Robin Headlam Wells and Johnjoe McFadden

The human nature debate

Why does the question of human nature arouse such passionate feelings? Does it make any practical difference whether we subscribe to one view of humankind or another?

Human nature has always divided intellectuals, and their different views of humanity have led to radically opposed answers to the question of what is most likely to lead to a just society. Optimists incline to the belief that human beings are innately beneficent and that it's civilization that has contaminated our natural goodness; pessimists believe that, because our nature is flawed – either by some mythical event such as the Fall, or as a consequence of the instincts that we have inherited from our hominid ancestors – we need the restraining influence of civilization to curb our natural propensity for wickedness. Such disagreements have probably existed for as long as people have speculated about their own nature. Underlying these disputes was the assumption that there is some kind of universal essence of human nature that links people in different times and different cultures as members of a single species. The question at issue was whether human beings in their primal state were fundamentally good, naturally inclined to evil, or perhaps a bit of both. That the question should have aroused strong feelings isn't surprising. If you believe that human beings are intrinsically good, you will probably be in favour of minimal interference in our lives from the state; if you believe that we inherit from our ancestral psyche not just an instinct for sociability but also a propensity for violence, you may incline towards a more interventionist state.

But in the modern world the focus of the dispute has shifted. What divides present-day thinkers is not a matter of different interpretations of human nature – though those still exist – but the question of whether or not it's meaningful to talk about human nature at all.

While humanist scientists and philosophers believe that an understanding of human nature must be the starting point for any responsible thinking about social policy, postmodernists argue that the very
notion of a universal human nature is a damaging form of ideological
mystification: under the guise of a benevolent concern for the good
of all humankind, the real purpose of the human nature myth is to
impose one particular set of male Eurocentric values on to the rest of
the world. In reality, it's argued, human nature is infinitely malleable.
The way we behave, the way we think, even our gender – all this is
purely a matter of social conditioning and owes nothing to our biological nature. Anti-essentialism – the belief that there is no such
thing as a universal essence of human nature – is a core principle in
much modern literary theory. As one distinguished American critic
explains, the key to what is new in postmodern literary criticism is 'the
basic issue of what one assumes to be the nature of man'; central to
the new criticism is 'the attack on the notion that man possesses a
transhistorical core of being. Rather, everything from "maternal
instinct" to conceptions of the self are now seen to be the products of
specific discourses and social processes.'[1]

Thus the old question: 'what can literature tell us about human
nature?' has now been replaced by a new question: if the very notion
of human nature is in doubt, can science resolve the conundrum that
divides humanists and postmodernists? Though sociobiologists and
evolutionary psychologists believe that we inherit certain neurobio-
logical traits that predispose us to see the world in a particular way and
to learn certain behaviours in preference to others,[2] modern scientists
are by no means agreed that it's meaningful to talk of a unified human
nature. These are the issues that speakers debated at the 2004 symposium on 'Literature, Science and Human Nature' at the Institute of
Contemporary Arts in London. But first let's put the modern debate
in context and consider the genesis of the opposition between
humanism and postmodernism.

Holding the mirror up to nature

Postmodern anti-humanism has its origins in an ideological opposition to Enlightenment thought. During the Enlightenment, poets
and philosophers set themselves the goal of ridding the world of
prejudice, dogma and superstition. They wanted to liberate the world
from tyranny and servitude. They believed in the principle of universal human rights. They campaigned for the abolition of slavery.
Appalled by what the Marquis de Condorcet called 'our treachery, our
murderous contempt for men of another colour or creed',[3] they aimed
to extend enlightened principles to every corner of the globe. Their
ideal was, in Condorcet's words, 'abolition of inequality between
nations, and the progress of equality within nations'.[4] The English
revolutionary Tom Paine summed up the Enlightenment belief in the
concept of human rights based on a universal core of essential
humanity when he wrote:

> Every history of the creation, and every traditionary account, whether
> from the lettered or unlettered world, however they may vary in their
> opinion or belief of certain particulars, all agree in establishing one point,
> *the unity of man*, by which I mean that men are all of *one degree*, and con-
> sequently, that all men are born equal, and with equal natural right.[5]

Enlightenment thinkers argued that progress towards a more just
world must be based on a sound knowledge of human nature.
Following Cicero,[6] they claimed that if humanity is ever to agree on
universal principles of social justice, that consensus must be sought,
not in some transcendent spiritual order, but in the facts of human
nature. 'How shall we begin to know the source of inequality between
men, if we do not begin by knowing mankind', wrote Jean-Jacques
Rousseau in his *Discourse on the Origin of Inequality* (1755). He argued
that without a true knowledge of human nature we will never understand the causes of human cruelty, social inequality, or the exploitation of one class by another.[7]

Inspired by the scientific revolution of the seventeenth century,
Enlightenment thinkers argued that an empirical approach to the

problem of human nature was more likely to lead to true knowledge of ourselves than appeals to tradition or authority. In his *A Treatise on Human Nature* (1739–40) David Hume claimed that knowledge of human nature was the foundation of all the sciences.[8] Hume believed that if we are to have a new science of humankind, it must be built on 'experience and observation'; any attempt to understand human nature that is not based on empirical observation is 'presumptuous and chimerical'.[9] Despite his Romantic belief in the importance of inspiration from the natural world, Rousseau too held that we should adopt a scientific approach to the study of human nature. He argued that, since the very idea of universal rights depends on understanding human beings and their needs, we must ask ourselves 'what experiments would have to be made, to discover the natural man'.[10]

In the modern world humanist thinkers continue to argue that an understanding of human nature must inform all responsible social policy. As A. C. Grayling puts it, 'Before one can get far with thinking about the good for humankind, one has to have a view about human nature, for the simple and obvious reason that a theory about the human good that drew only on consideration about what, say, dogs and horses are like (and what dogs and horses like) would be of exceedingly limited use.'[11]

Literature is of particular interest to humanist thinkers because of what they believe it can tell us about ourselves as human beings. Poets, dramatists and novelists have traditionally been seen as exceptionally gifted observers of human nature. John Dryden defined a play as 'a just and lively image of human nature, representing its passions and humours, and the changes of fortune to which it is subject'.[12] A century later Jane Austen described the novel as 'a work in which the most thorough knowledge of human nature, the happiest delineation of its varieties, the liveliest effusions of wit and humour are conveyed to the world in the best chosen language'.[13] Both were part of an ancient humanist tradition that valued literature for what it could tell us about humankind. By holding the mirror up to our nature (as Hamlet puts it) and showing us the characteristic virtues and vices of our species, literature, so the argument went, could give us a much better insight into humankind than any philosophical treatise could do.[14] When Enlightenment poets and philosophers proclaimed, in Alexander Pope's words, that 'the proper study of mankind is man'[15] they were echoing the belief of Renaissance humanists in the power of literature to instruct us in the ways of human nature. The zoologist Edward O. Wilson offers a modern, neo-Darwinist's version of the old belief, shared by Renaissance and Enlightenment humanists alike, in the universal subject matter of literature when he writes: 'Works of art that prove enduring are intensely humanistic. Born in the imagination of individuals, they nevertheless touch upon what was universally endowed by human evolution.'[16]

Modern humanists argue that, by enabling us to make imaginative contact with other minds in worlds remote historically or culturally from our own, literature can help us to appreciate that our common humanity is more important than the ethnic and religious differences that create so much havoc in our lives. As one critic puts it, 'one of the satisfactions afforded by literature is to be found in the way it allows readers to recognize as a part of common humanity feelings which they had previously regarded as individual or private'.[17] In that way, humanists believe, literature can encourage those central principles of Enlightenment thought – sympathy, understanding and toleration.

Postmodernism and the challenge to Enlightenment rationalism

The Enlightenment has always had its opponents. In rejecting Reformation Christianity's emphasis on the depravity of human nature, some Enlightenment thinkers went to the opposite extreme and claimed that, since human beings are inherently reasonable creatures, all you have to do is show people the truth and they will naturally follow it. 'Vice is contrary to the nature of man, as man; for it is contrary to the order of reason, the peculiar and highest principle in man', wrote the philosopher Benjamin Whichcote in 1703.[18] It was such absurdly optimistic claims for the reasonableness of humankind that Jonathan Swift attacked in his satirical pamphlet *A Modest Proposal* (1729). How shall we alleviate the scandalous poverty that afflicts our nation, asks Swift's fictional author and would-be philanthropist? The truly shocking thing about his solution – that the Irish might solve their economic problems by breeding children for the table – is not the almost ludicrous barbarity of his proposal, but the fact that seemingly rational individuals can be so blind to the human consequences of their reasoning. It's not fanciful to suggest that it was a similar kind of reasoning that led to the greatest crime against humanity in recorded history.

Swift was attacking not reason itself, but the abuse of reason. Since human beings are the only species capable of rational thought, it's true to say that reason is one of the defining features of our humanity. But deny the fact that emotion is an equally important part of our makeup – neuroscientists claim that the architecture of the human brain shows that 'passion is inseverably linked to reason'[19] – and you are in danger of producing the sort of brutally callous economic policies that Swift satirized in *A Modest Proposal*, the utilitarian educational system that Dickens parodied in *Hard Times*, or even the Holocaust itself.

However, in the twentieth century some thinkers went further and argued, not just that it's dangerous to ignore the emotional dimension of our lives, but that there's something destructive in the very nature of reason itself. A long tradition going back at least as far as Wordsworth's Preface to *The Lyrical Ballads* had contrasted life in the modern world with the imagined harmony of a pre-industrial age. But during the Second World War members of the Frankfurt School of philosophers and social commentators claimed that the horrors of the modern world were traceable directly to the baleful influence of the Enlightenment. 'The fully enlightened earth radiates disaster triumphant', wrote Theodor Adorno and Max Horkheimer in their influential *Dialectic of Enlightenment* (1944).[20] A central theme in their book was the growing power of the state to control people's minds: though the Enlightenment may have liberated humanity from superstition, the scientific rationalism that it unleashed has since been used to inflict a far more insidious kind of enslavement of our minds. When science destroyed the gods of the old animistic world, it replaced them with the technology that now controls our lives. The result, Adorno and Horkheimer believed, was 'the total schematization of men'.[21]

Another member of the Frankfurt School, Herbert Marcuse, also saw instrumental reason as the bane of modern life. In his influential *One Dimensional Man* (1964) he argued that the 'technological rationality' that was the Enlightenment's legacy to the modern world had become a means of endorsing and consolidating the interests of 'the powers that be'.[22] The modern state might have abandoned the threat of physical punishment in favour of technology as a way of controlling our minds, but its power has not diminished. On the contrary, 'the scope of society's domination over the individual is immeasurably greater than ever before'.[23] Like Adorno and Horkheimer, Marcuse believed that blame for the ills of a society that specialized in the control of people's minds lay not with individuals, but with 'the power of the system'. The phrase that summed up his despairing view of the modern world was a remark by Roland Barthes that he chose as one of his chapter epigraphs: 'In the present state of history, all political writing can only confirm a police-universe.'[24] For Marcuse, as for Adorno and Horkheimer, the legacy that the Enlightenment bequeathed to the modern world has been an unmitigated disaster. Such is the power of 'the system' that the 'police-universe' is able now to control, not just our bodies, but our innermost thoughts.

Like Adorno and Horkheimer, Marcuse deplored the dehumanizing nature of modern post-industrial society. But it was Michel Foucault's critique of the Enlightenment that caught the imaginations of postmodern literary critics. It has traditionally been assumed that the social reforms of the eighteenth century were, in part at least, a product of the liberal ideals of the Enlightenment *philosophes*. If mockery of the insane was no longer thought to be a proper form of social entertainment for civilized men and women, that was due in part to the new climate of enlightened opinion; if criminals were no longer subjected to public dismemberment, that was because people had learned a new respect for human rights. Foucault challenged this view of the Enlightenment. In *The Birth of the Clinic* (1963) he argued that, far from marking a new sympathy for society's outcasts and affording protection from casual abuse, asylums for the insane were an attempt by the state to control the minds of its subjects. In *Discipline and Punish* (1975) he suggested that the new criminal system with its emphasis on reform rather than retributive punishment disguised a darker purpose. The monstrous brutalities of the *ancien régime* might have gone; but they had been replaced by something far more sinister: 'what was emerging was . . . not so much a new respect for the humanity of the condemned as a tendency towards a closer penal mapping of the social body'.[25] In short, the supposed humanitarian reforms of the eighteenth century were actually a means of creating and controlling obedient servants of 'the system'.

In *Discipline and Punish* Foucault tells us that he is writing 'the history of the present'.[26] He is concerned, in other words, to uncover the historical processes that led, not just to our present penal system, but to those 'mechanisms of normalization' by which the state shapes our minds and controls our thoughts. Foucault was not warning his readers, as Aldous Huxley and George Orwell did, of the future dystopia to which present social policies were in danger of leading us. His aim was not to extrapolate from existing social tendencies and imagine what terrors we might stumble into in the future; his subject was the here and now, the horror of the normal, everyday world of laudable intentions, betrayed ideals and politicians' lies that we in the Western democracies thought we knew so well. The task he had set himself was to defamiliarize that world and expose the surveillance systems that control our lives so successfully that we are largely unaware of them. As Foucault saw it, modern society was like the world of the Wachowskis' *Matrix* films, a nightmare world of purely indifferent, impersonal malevolence.

Driving Foucault's assault on the Enlightenment was his belief that the notion of a resilient core of human nature was no more than a myth promulgated by 'the state'. In reality our thoughts, our emotions and what we believe to be our 'instincts' are created and controlled by 'the power of the system'. People imagine that there are certain human constants that transcend time and enable us to learn from the past; but in reality, wrote Foucault in an essay on Nietzsche, 'nothing in man is sufficiently stable to serve as a basis for understanding other men'.[27] We are all of us 'isolated within our own peculiar modalities of experience'.[28]

Though historians have contested Foucault's revisionist intellectual history of the post-Enlightenment world,[29] the assault on the Enlightenment and its ideals remains one of the founding principles of postmodern thought. 'Postmodernism views Enlightenment thought itself as the main source of the terrors and disorder of the modern world', explains one textbook on postmodernism.[30] At the core of postmodern literary theory is the belief that there is no universal essence of human nature. 'Constructionism', writes one leading Shakespeare scholar, 'is one of the basic propositions by which new historicism as a way of reading has distinguished itself from humanism. Where humanism assumes a core essence that unites people otherwise separated in time and social circumstances new historicism insists on cultural differences.'[31] What is true of new historicism is true of postmodern literary theory in general: human nature is a myth that the post-Enlightenment state has invented in order to control its subjects. Feminists are particularly suspicious of appeals to human nature. And with good reason. Throughout history men have denied women full legal rights on the grounds that they are inferior to men and unfitted by 'nature' to take a full part in civic or commercial life or to receive equal wages. Whether gender is exclusively a matter of social conditioning or owes something also to biologically determined predispositions remains a hotly contested issue.[32]

Literature in a postmodern world

How does all this affect our view of literature, the way it is produced and the way it affects our lives? For Renaissance and Enlightenment humanists self-knowledge was 'the chief part of wisdom'.[33] By that they meant that it is important that people should have an understanding both of humankind in general and of their own particular strengths and weaknesses as individuals.[34] Because great writers were thought to have an intuitive grasp of what makes human beings tick, literature could help us to understand our humanity. For postmodernists this is doubly misleading. It is not just that the notion of a universal human nature is a myth with no foundation in reality; the idea of an inner self is also a spurious invention of the modern world. If capitalist ideology emphasizes the value of personal autonomy and individual freedom, so the argument goes, that is because it requires complicit, obedient subjects who willingly accept their subjection. In constructing us as its subjects, and persuading us that we are autonomous individuals blessed with free will and capable of making rational choices, ideology works in such a way as to obscure the oppression that Foucault believed was the real driving force in all human relations. For postmodernists, the notion of essential selfhood is 'epistemologically insupportable'.[35]

If the self is a chimera, that means that any idea of creative originality has limited meaning. In his seminal essay 'The Death of the Author' (1968) Roland Barthes famously declared that 'it is language which speaks, not the author', by which he meant that the power of ideology to shape our thoughts is far greater, not just than we are prepared to admit, but than we are even aware of. In reality, Barthes claimed, the writer has no passions, humours, feelings, impressions; he is merely a repository of words and phrases culled from other writers; his 'only power is to mix [pre-existing] writings'.[36] Popularizing these ideas, Terence Hawkes explains that

> one of the major effects of latter-day post-structuralist thinking has been the subversion of a central ideological commitment to the idea of the individual, sovereign self, the human subject, as the fundamental unit of existence and the main negotiable instrument of meaning. In consequence, the notion of the text as the direct expression of that subject's innermost thoughts and feelings has also been abandoned.[37]

William Hazlitt said that original genius is nothing but nature and feeling working in the artist's mind;[38] postmodernism says that it's nothing but ideology working in *our* minds.

If the idea of an autonomous, inner self is an illusion, then any thought of reaching out to minds in other cultures or of empathizing with the predicaments of people in social worlds quite different from our own is also illusory. Foucault argued that once it becomes clear that there are no human constants that transcend time and link us with the past, we have to accept that the most that historians can do is expose that radical discontinuity: 'History becomes "effective" to the degree that it introduces discontinuity into our very being.'[39] As with history, so with literature. If postmodernism is right and there is no such thing as a universal human nature; if we are indeed 'isolated within our own peculiar modalities of experience', then we have to accept that literature too is emptied of any moral or social value. Just as postmodern historiographers deny that history can ever give us 'an informed appreciation of the predicaments and viewpoints of people in the past',[40] so if you strip literature of the universal 'passions and humours' that Dryden thought were the subject of drama, you are left with no means of evaluating literature from another age or another culture. As Terry Eagleton explains, for the postmodernist 'There is no such thing as a literary work or tradition which is valuable in itself, regardless of what anyone might have said or come to say about it.'[41] The result is a world in which 'everything exists [and] nothing has value', in the words of E. M. Forster's Mrs Moore.[42]

From Descartes to Darwin

Though writers, philosophers and social scientists have been denying the existence of an essential core of humanity for the best part of a century, the debate on human nature has now entered a new phase. Modern science's engagement with human nature can be traced back to the Enlightenment, when reason rather than revelation or tradition finally came to dominate the natural sciences. But did 'nature' include humanity? The earliest scientists and philosophers were ambivalent. In René Descartes' mechanistic philosophy the world was divided into matter and mind. Descartes proposed that animals were made of matter – elaborate machines, different in complexity but not in prin-ciple, from the fairground automata of his day. This in itself was a rev-olutionary step because it placed the examination of living creatures outside the domain of religion, allowing their study to become a secular science. But even Descartes could not accept that humans were no different, in principle, from a cuckoo clock, so he proposed *dualism*, the theory that although the human body is made of matter and driven by corporeal pulleys, pumps and levers, our conscious actions are driven by a spiritual soul. Descartes even went on to propose a seat for the soul in the tiny pineal gland deep in the brain (he couldn't accept a duplicated soul and it was the only structure he could find in the brain that wasn't duplicated across the hemispheres). It was this soul, with its higher feelings and direct connection to the divine that was, in Descartes' philosophy, the source of human nature and what separated us from lowly animals.

There were, of course, problems with dualism, most famously the nature of the causal connection between an ethereal soul and a phys-ical body: the *mind–body problem*. Yet dualism was a great asset to the pioneer biologists since it allowed them to study the mechanisms of the natural world without treading on the sensitive toes of religious orthodoxy. Linnaeus could begin the monumental task of classifying nature by gathering all living creatures under a single binomial umbrella; Hunter could dissect the sinews of corpses to reveal human anatomy; Louis Pasteur could peer into the microscopic world and discover the hidden agents of disease. All these enterprises could proceed without incurring the wrath of the Church because most biologists remained committed dualists, content to unravel the mechanisms of the world but not daring to investigate the device that performed the unravelling.

The first chink in the dualist armour came with the recognition that the gap between animals and us was not so great after all. When Darwin's apes climbed down from the trees they brought with them all those mechanisms that were assumed to drive animal behaviour. It wasn't long before scientists started to think the previously unthinkable. If humankind had once been a mechanistic animal, was it likely that they had left all those mechanisms up in the trees? Perhaps the stream of consciousness itself may have a physical rather than a spiritual source?

Scientific dualism quickly went the way of spontaneous generation, vitalism and other theories that sought to explain the wonders of the natural world by inserting a magical, spiritual or mystical ingredient. With Darwin's publication of *The Descent of Man* in 1871 and *The Expression of Emotions in Man and Animals* in the following year the way was cleared for a fully scientific enquiry into the nature of human nature. Humanity, the creator of science, also became its subject.

Eugenics

But then came eugenics. Rarely covered in textbooks, eugenics is biology's dirty secret. Although its roots go deep – at least as far back as Plato's *Republic* – there is no doubt that its popularity in the late nineteenth and early twentieth century owed much to its supposed scientific credentials within the framework of Darwinian natural selection.[43] Survival of the fittest is of course eugenics *au naturel*. Darwin recognized that the consequences of Nature's eugenics policy over thousands of generations was evolution. Darwin himself (perhaps deeply affected by the loss of his own daughter four years earlier) lamented natural selection's 'clumsy, wasteful, blundering, low, and horribly cruel' action.[44] But if human nature was malleable and could be shaped by Nature, couldn't man do better? Many of Darwin's contemporaries, such as his cousin the geneticist Francis Galton, sought to improve on natural selection with programmes that promoted breeding of those who possessed 'goodness of constitution, of physique and mental capacity'. From its inception, the eugenics movement was openly racist, with the aim of ensuring that the 'feeble nations' give way before the 'nobler varieties of mankind'. There was never any doubt as to the identity of the 'nobler varieties', who were of course the white Anglo-Saxon middle- and upper-class intellectuals who thronged into the eugenics society meeting rooms.

The blame for the eugenics movement cannot, however, be laid solely at the door of the scientific establishment. Eugenics may have been the bastard progeny of the theory of natural selection, but the infant pseudoscience was enthusiastically adopted by many of the leading intellectuals, writers, politicians, economists and social reformers of the day. In November 1913 the Oxford University Union carried a motion by 105 votes to 66 that 'this house approves the principles of eugenics'. As a cabinet minister, the young Winston Churchill advocated compulsory sterilization of 'the feeble minded and insane classes'. H. G. Wells frequently promoted eugenics. George Bernard Shaw wrote, 'being cowards, we defeat natural selection under cover of philanthropy: being sluggards, we neglect artificial selection under cover of delicacy and morality'.[45] In 1915 Virginia Woolf wrote in her diary:

> On the towpath we met & had to pass a long line of imbeciles. The first was a very tall young man, just queer enough to look twice at, but no more; the second shuffled, & looked aside; & then one realised that every one in that long line was a miserable ineffective shuffling idiotic creature, with no forehead, or no chin, & an imbecile grin, or a wild suspicious stare. It was perfectly horrible. They should certainly be killed.[46]

In truth, popular support for eugenics amongst the West European and US intelligentsia had very little to do with its dubious scientific credentials. Its wellsprings were far more to do with the middle- and upper-class fear of the burgeoning populations of the poor. For Churchill's 'insane classes' read working classes, and when Francis Galton advocated breeding from 'those only of the best stock', it was obvious to everyone who was to be left out. The contraception pioneer Marie Stopes campaigned to pass laws to enable sterilization of the 'the diseased', the 'racially negligent' and 'the feeble minded'.[47]

Many European countries and US states adopted eugenicist sterilization policies. Even in liberal Sweden, more than 62,000 people (mostly women) with physical or mental handicap, or considered merely to be socially 'undesirable', were sterilized against their will. The full horrors of eugenicist policies were realized in the 1934 German racial hygiene law that led to the enforced sterilization of more than 80,000 individuals considered by the 'hereditary health courts' to be 'lives unworthy of life'. Although in reality only peripheral to the terrors of Nazi Germany, Hitler's enthusiastic support of its principles as a means of engineering the master race established eugenics as the pariah of post-war science.

With the discrediting of eugenics in the years following the Second World War, any scientific investigation of the biological roots of human nature took a similar fall from grace. Behavioural biologists retreated into the forest to study chimpanzees, ants, or monkeys, and the field of study of human social behaviour was left to anthropologists and sociologists. A new dualism emerged, with culture replacing Descartes' soul as the primary mover of the human mind.

Genes versus culture

As discussed by Steven Pinker in this volume, the principle that dominated enquiry into human nature in the post-war years was the 'blank slate', the concept that the mind of man (uniquely among animals) was essentially free of biological constraints. Sexual inclination, intelligence, personality and character were all claimed to be the products of culture, rather than biology. The argument was bolstered by the fact that many key aspects of human social behaviour, such as altruism, appeared, on the face of it, to be contrary to the predictions of the theory of natural selection. As Darwin himself lamented, it is the struggle (for survival) between individuals that dominates the natural world; but cooperation rather than competition is the cornerstone of all human cultures. The structure of DNA was elucidated in 1953, but despite the realization that genes encoded the form of the brain, its significance for understanding how the human mind worked was generally considered to be minimal.

The blank-slate view of a human nature entirely free of the shackles of biology persisted for several decades. But in the latter years of the twentieth century the slate became increasingly marked by the

scratchings of neurobiologists, sociobiologists, behavioural psychologists and geneticists. Edward O. Wilson was amongst the first to
pick up the chalk with the publication of *Sociobiology: The New
Synthesis* in 1975.[48] Wilson's book explored new evolutionary
insights (by himself, Robert Trivers, John Maynard Smith and many
other biologists) into the social behaviours of animals, and by extension, humanity. A year later Richard Dawkins published *The Selfish
Gene*[49] in which he provided a genocentric view of the entire realm
of biology. Animal social behaviours, such as altruism, now yielded
to genocentric theories such as kin selection and reciprocal altruism.
If genes could persuade animals like bats to be kind to strangers then
it became increasingly difficult to argue that they could not similarly
be involved in human altruism.

Alongside advances in theoretical biology came genetic studies
that demonstrated inherited components to relatively common
behavioural conditions, such as autism or schizophrenia.[50] Gene
involvement in mental capacity had already been accepted for
genetic diseases such as Down's syndrome. But Down's syndrome
(which is usually caused by the inheritance of three, rather than two,
copies of chromosome twenty-one) was considered an extreme
genetic condition with no relevance to the normal population. In
contrast, autism and schizophrenia exhibit spectrums of disease that
range from the extremely dysfunctional to people who lead relatively
normal lives. Genes appeared to be involved all the way along the
spectrum, implying that genes affected the way apparently *normal*
people thought. Neurobiologists and psychologists entered the fray
with the demonstration that lesions in particular regions of the
brain caused behavioural disturbances such as aggression, hyperactivity, depression or cognitive defects such as the visual agnosia
experienced by the eponymous patient of Oliver Sacks' book, *The
Man Who Mistook His Wife For a Hat*.[51] Once again, the spectrum of
dysfunction overlapped with the range of behaviour found in apparently normal people, suggesting that a good deal of the natural variation in humankind sprang from physical rather than cultural
causes.

Yet, despite these developments, academics and critics in the social sciences and humanities – the traditional home for those interested in the study of humankind – remained either deeply sceptical or openly hostile to any mechanistic account of human nature. The tone was set nearly a century ago by George Bernard Shaw who wrote to Henry James,

> In the name of human vitality WHERE is the charm in that useless, dispiriting, discouraging fatalism which broke out so horribly in the eighteen-sixties at the word of Darwin, and persuaded people in spite of their own teeth and claws that Man is the will-less slave and victim of his environment? What is the use of writing plays? – what is the use of any-thing? – if there is not a Will that finally moulds chaos itself into a race of gods with heaven for an environment, and if that Will is not incarnated in man . . .[52]

Half a century later, C. P. Snow lamented the continuing divide between the sciences and the humanities in his lecture on *The Two Cultures*. And though postmodernism has largely discarded Shaw's 'Will' as a component of human nature, it remains equally hostile to biological explanation of the way we are.

The basic tenet of the scientific approach is that there is an objective reality out there for science to uncover. In this view, science occupies a special place among human endeavours in that its 'truths' should float free of the belief systems of the scientists who establish them: Newton's laws of gravity should be just as true to an Australian aborigine or an Inuit Indian as they were for an English gentleman. But though a reasonable case can be made for the laws of physics, immutability of the laws of the natural world is much less certain. The history of eugenics should perhaps give pause to any geneticist claiming overarching truths; but when in June 2000 Francis Collins announced the near completion of the Human Genome Project at a White House reception, he proclaimed 'We have caught the first glimpse of our own instruction book, previously known only to God.'[53] This claim for scientific objectivity standing outside of culture was questioned as far back as Karl Marx, who wrote to Engels that

'It is remarkable how Darwin rediscovers, among the beasts and plants, the society of England with its division of labour, competition, opening up of new markets, "inventions" and Malthusian "struggle for existence" '.[54] In this volume, Catherine Belsey notes a similar match between the functionalist description of human nature and the modern suburban lifestyles of the (mostly male) scientists who promote sociobiology theories. And it can hardly be a coincidence that the debate on the validity of gene-centred theories of human nature has tended to separate scientists into camps that reflect their political views as accurately as their scientific ones. It seems that the political affiliation of scientists is an important influence on their critical assessment of scientific theories.

Postmodernists argue that the language through which science is communicated inevitably leaves a trail of cultural baggage. A gene may have an objective reality, but a 'selfish gene' is a construct that depends on the culturally loaded meaning of the term 'selfish'. 'Gene' itself means different things to different scientists who vary widely in the degree of genetic control that they are prepared to accept for these entities. So how can any theory of genes be universally true if its truth is conditional on the meaning of its terms? The philosopher Dan Dennett coined the term 'greedy reductionism' to describe the habit of some scientists of relentlessly reducing explanations down to the smallest possible level, in this case, genes. Most notoriously, Herrnstein and Murray published *The Bell Curve*[55] in 1994 arguing that genetic differences in intelligence accounted for most of the economic inequality in American society: if you are poor it's probably because you are stupid. *The Bell Curve* was greeted with howls of protest and Herrnstein and Murray were claimed to be 'academic Nazis' and closet eugenicists. Many fellow sociobiologists came to be tarred with the same brush and were accused of racism, sexism and homophobia. Public-speaking engagements in the US were often marred by verbal abuse and mass walkouts. More recently, the efforts of the Human Genome Diversity Project (HGDP) to collect DNA from the full range of human variability has been halted in its tracks by suspicions, particularly among many native people, that the true intention of the project was a kind of postcolonial genetic exploitation rather than rational science.

So a 'gene' may be a piece of DNA, a unit of heredity or a tool of exploitation. Its influence could be profound or trivial, depending on your viewpoint. Yet despite the uncertainties over their precise nature, they have continued to be implicated as causes of human nature. With the sequencing of the human genome in the closing years of the twentieth century scientists were presented with approximately 32,000 genes and as many as half of them were likely to be involved in brain development and function. Few scientists would argue today that all this genetic inheritance has absolutely no role to play in the way our brain works.

A posthuman future?

The arguments rage on, with both sides mostly talking past each other. The debate would have only academic interest were it not for the fact that genetic engineering, human cloning and gene therapy are likely to provide the tools that nineteenth- and twentieth-century eugenicists lacked: the ability to engineer human nature. The coming decades will probably see successful gene therapy developed for lethal genetic diseases, such as cystic fibrosis or muscular dystrophy. But the same tools may be applied to those conditions, such as autism or schizophrenia, where dysfunction flows smoothly into normality and even genius. Should we – could we – engineer minds free of schizophrenia or autism at the risk of losing some of the range of human variability that has given us brilliant poets, writers, artists or scientists? What of aggression, which has been similarly linked (though not nearly as convincingly) to genes? Or hyperactivity, or low intelligence, or gender choice? Or what about positive attributes, like high intelligence or creativity, if these are found to have inherited components? IVF clinics already offer prospective mothers a selection of attributes in their sperm donors. Reproductive clinics of the future may be able to offer extra doses of intelligence or creativity genes to their clients (at a price, of course). Nearly all of us want our children to be clever, talented, successful, and with tastes and ethics broadly similar to our own, but would we be prepared to load the genetic dice to achieve these aims? What is the prognosis for human nature if it does indeed yield to genetic tinkering?

And what of reason? The scientific age was initiated by the Age of Reason. But as Catherine Belsey asks in this volume, can science, the product of reason, unpick its own cause? And where is Shaw's 'Will' (if it exists) located in all those neurons and genes? Are we slaves to reason, to our genes or to our culture?

Most scientists admit they are not necessarily the best people to answer these questions. The modern scientific mind is generally focused on detail and the particular rather than the broad sweeps required to encompass the range and complexity of human nature. It is surely in the products of the humanities, great literature and the arts that the quest to understand human nature has reached its highest expression. Yet, as discussed earlier, most of the humanities, and particularly the discipline of literary criticism, remain deeply hostile to any attempt to bring genes into any discussion of human behaviour or culture. And the fact that *The Da Vinci Code* has outsold all books on the genetic code many times over is a sobering reflection of the position of science in the minds of most readers.

Promoting some kind of dialogue between writers, literary critics and scientists was the purpose of the 2004 symposium on 'Literature, Science and Human Nature'. The meeting was so successful that we felt we could not allow it to pass without making a record of its achievements available to all those who couldn't make it to the meeting: hence this volume. The chapters are arranged around the session topics addressed by the speakers: 'Is human nature written in our genes or in our books?', 'Can science and literature collaborate to define human nature?', 'What has biology got to do with imagination?', 'Do we need a theory of human nature to tell us how to act?'

What is remarkable is that, despite their differences, enthusiasts on both sides of the cultural divide found that they had much that they could agree on. Points of disagreement, and there are many, remain.

Yet there was, and is in this volume, a real attempt to reach out across the chasm that separates the two cultures to reach a better understanding of what it means to be human.

Notes

1. Jean Howard, 'The New Historicism in Renaissance Studies', *English Literary Renaissance*, 16 (1986), p. 20.

2. See Edward O. Wilson, *Consilience: The Unity of Knowledge* (London: Little, Brown, 1998), p. 164.

3. *Sketch for a Historical Picture of the Progress of the Human Mind*, in Peter Gay (ed.), *The Enlightenment: A Comprehensive Anthology* (New York: Simon & Schuster, 1973), p. 805.

4. *The Progress of the Mind*, in Gay, p. 803.

5. Tom Paine, *The Rights of Man, Common Sense, and Other Political Writings* (1791), ed. Mark Philp (Oxford and New York: Oxford University Press, 1995), p. 117.

6. See Marcus Tullius Cicero, *De legibus*, trans. Clinton Walker Keyes, Loeb Classical Library (London: Heinemann, 1948), pp. 315–17.

7. Preface to *Discourse on the Origin of Inequality*, in Gay, *The Enlightenment*, p. 181.

8. Introduction to *A Treatise on Human Nature*, in Gay, *The Enlightenment*, p. 483.

9. *A Treatise on Human Nature*, p. 487.

10. Preface to *Discourse on the Origin of Inequality*, in Gay, *The Enlightenment*, p. 183.

11. A. C. Grayling, *What is Good? The Search for the Best Way to Live* (London: Weidenfeld & Nicolson, 2003), p. 210.

12. *Of Dramatic Poesy and Other Critical Essays*, ed. George Watson, 2 vols (London and New York: Dent, 1962), Vol. 1, p. 25.

13. Jane Austen, *Northanger Abbey*, ed. K. M. Lobb (London: University of London Press, 1956), p. 65.

14. See, for example, Sir Philip Sidney, *An Apology for Poetry*, ed. Geoffrey Shepherd (London: Nelson, 1965), p. 108.

15. *An Essay on Man*, II.2, *The Poems of Alexander Pope*, ed. John Butt (London: Methuen, 1963), p. 516.

16. *Consilience*, p. 243.

17. Richard Webster, *Why Freud Was Wrong: Sin, Science and Psychoanalysis*, rev. edn (London: HarperCollins, 1996), p. 480.

18. *Moral and Religious Aphorisms*, No. 212, quoted by A. R. Humphreys, *The Augustan World: Life and Letters in Eighteenth-Century England*, 2nd edn (London: Methuen, 1964), p. 191.

19. Wilson, *Consilience*, p. 116.

20. Theodor W. Adorno and Max Horkheimer, *Dialectic of Enlightenment*, trans. John Cumming (London: Allen Lane, 1973), p. 3.

21. *Dialectic of Enlightenment*, p. 35.

22. Herbert Marcuse, *One Dimensional Man: Studies in the Ideology of Advanced Industrial Society* (London: Routledge & Kegan Paul, 1964), pp. 15–16, 18.

23. *One Dimensional Man*, p. x.

24. Quoted in *One Dimensional Man*, p. 84.

25. Michel Foucault, *Discipline and Punish: The Birth of the Prison*, trans. Alan Sheridan (London: Allen Lane, 1977), p. 78.

26. *Discipline and Punish*, p. 31.

27. Michel Foucault, 'Nietzsche, Genealogy, History', *Language, Counter-Memory, Practice*, ed. and trans. Donald F. Bouchard (Oxford: Blackwell, 1977), p. 153.

28. This phrase is from a tribute essay on Foucault by his disciple, the postmodern historiographer Hayden White ('Foucault Decoded: Notes from Underground', in *Tropics of Discourse: Essays in Cultural Criticism* (Baltimore, MD: Johns Hopkins University Press, 1985), p. 234).

29. J. G. Merquior, *Foucault*, 2nd edn (London: Fontana, 1991), p. 102.

30. Patricia Waugh, *Practising Postmodernism/Reading Modernism* (London and New York: Edward Arnold, 1992), p. 69.

31. Bruce Smith, *Shakespeare and Masculinity* (Oxford: Oxford University Press, 2000), pp. 131–2.

32. For two opposing modern views of gender see Judith Butler, *Gender Trouble: Feminism and the Subversion of Identity* (New York: Routledge,

1990) and Anne Campbell, *A Mind of Her Own: The Evolutionary Psychology of Women* (Oxford: Oxford University Press, 2002).

33. Desiderius Erasmus, *Enchiridion militis christiani: An English Version*, ed. Anne M. O'Donnell, SND (Oxford: Early English Text Society, 1981), p. 59.

34. The Elizabethan psychologist Thomas Wright wrote: '[self-knowledge] consisteth of a perfect experience every man hath of himself in particular, and an universal knowledge of men's inclinations in common' (*The Passions of the Mind in General* (1601), ed. William Webster Newbold (New York and London: Garland, 1986), pp. 92–3).

35. Linda Charnes, *Notorious Identity: Materializing the Subject in Shakespeare* (Cambridge, MA: Harvard University Press, 1993), p. 10.

36. Roland Barthes, 'The Death of the Author', *Image Music Text*, trans. Stephen Heath (London: Fontana, 1977), pp. 142–3, 146.

37. *Meaning by Shakespeare* (London: Routledge, 1992), p. 5.

38. 'On Genius and Common Sense', *Table Talk* (London: Dent, 1908), p. 43.

39. Foucault, 'Nietzsche, Genealogy, History', pp. 153–4.

40. Keith Jenkins, *Re-thinking History* (London and New York: Routledge, 1991), p. 48.

41. *Literary Theory: An Introduction* (Oxford: Blackwell, 1983), p. 11.

42. *A Passage to India* (1924; repr. Melbourne, London and Baltimore, MD: Penguin, 1936), p. 147.

43. G. K. Chesterton, *Eugenics and Other Evils* (Seattle: Inkling Books, 2003).

44. Richard Dawkins, *A Devil's Chaplain* (London: Weidenfeld & Nicolson, 2003).

45. George Bernard Shaw, Epistle Dedicatory, 'To Arthur Bingham Walkley', *Man and Superman* (1903; repr. Harmondsworth: Penguin Books, 1946), p. 25.

46. *The Diary of Virginia Woolf*, ed. Anne Olivier Bell, 5 vols (London: Hogarth Press, 1977), Vol. 1 (1915–19), p. 13.

47. Ruth Hall, *Marie Stopes: A Biography* (London: Virago Press, 1978), p. 180.

48. Edward O. Wilson, *Sociobiology: The New Synthesis* (Cambridge, MA: Harvard University Press, 2000).

49. Richard Dawkins, *The Selfish Gene* (Oxford: Oxford University Press, 1976).

50. Matt Ridley, *Genome: The Autobiography of a Species in 23 Chapters* (London: Fourth Estate, 1999).

51. Oliver Sacks, *The Man Who Mistook His Wife for a Hat* (London: Duckworth, 1986), p. 10.

52. George Bernard Shaw, *Collected Letters*, ed. Dan H. Laurence, 4 vols (London: Max Reinhardt, 1988), Vol. 2 (1898–1910), p. 827.

53. Colin Macilwain, 'World Leaders Heap Praise on Human Genome Landmark', *Nature* 405 (29 June 2000), p. 984.

54. *Selected Correspondence of Karl Marx and Friedrich Engels*, trans. I. Lasker, ed. S. W. Ryazanskawa (Moscow: Progress Publishers, 1975), p. 120.

55. Richard J. Herrnstein and Charles Murray, The *Bell Curve: Intelligence and Class Structure in American Life* (London: Simon & Schuster, 1996).

I   Is human nature written in our genes or in our books?

1   The biology of fiction

Steven Pinker

Man does not live by bread alone, nor by know-how, safety, children, or sex. People everywhere spend as much time as they can afford on activities that, in the struggle to survive and reproduce, seem pointless. In all cultures, people tell stories and recite poetry. They joke, laugh, and tease. They sing and dance. They decorate surfaces. They perform rituals. They wonder about the causes of fortune and misfortune, and hold beliefs about the supernatural that contradict everything else they know about the world. They concoct theories of the universe and their place within it.

As if that were not enough of a puzzle, the more biologically frivolous and vain the activity, the more people exalt it. Art, literature, music, wit, religion, and philosophy are thought to be not just pleasurable but noble. They are the mind's best work, what makes life worth living. Why do we pursue the trivial and futile and experience them as sublime? To many educated people the question seems horribly philistine, even immoral. But it is unavoidable for anyone interested in the biological makeup of *Homo sapiens*. Members of our species do mad deeds like taking vows of celibacy, living for their music, selling their blood to buy movie tickets, and going to graduate school. Why? How might we understand the psychology of the arts, humour, religion, and philosophy if, as I have argued elsewhere, the mind is a naturally selected neural computer?[1]

Every college has a faculty of arts, which usually dominates the institution in numbers and in the public eye. But the tens of thousands of scholars and millions of pages of scholarship have shed almost no light on the question of why people pursue the arts at all. The function of the arts is almost defiantly obscure, and I think there are several reasons why.

One is that the arts engage not only the psychology of aesthetics but the psychology of status. The very uselessness of art that makes it so incomprehensible to evolutionary biology makes it all too comprehensible to economics and social psychology. What better proof that you have money to spare than your being able to spend it on doodads and stunts that don't fill the belly or keep the rain out but that require precious materials, years of practice, a command of obscure texts, or intimacy with the elite? Thorstein Veblen's and Quentin Bell's analyses of taste and fashion, in which an elite's conspicuous displays of consumption, leisure, and outrage are emulated by the rabble, sending the elite off in search of new inimitable displays,[2] nicely explain the otherwise inexplicable oddities of the arts. The grand styles of one century become tacky in the next, as we see in words that are both period labels and terms of abuse (*gothic, mannerist, baroque, rococo*). The steadfast patrons of the arts are the aristocracy and those who want to join them. Most people would lose their taste for a musical recording if they learned it was being sold at supermarket checkout counters or on late-night television, and even the work of relatively prestigious artists, such as Pierre Auguste Renoir, draws derisive reviews when it is shown in a popular 'blockbuster' museum show. The value of art is largely unrelated to aesthetics: a priceless masterpiece becomes worthless if it is found to be a forgery; soup cans and comic strips become high art when the art world says they are, and then command conspicuously wasteful prices. Modern and postmodern works are intended not to give pleasure but to confirm or confound the theories of a guild of critics and analysts, to *épater la bourgeoisie*, or to baffle the rubes in Peoria.

The banality that the psychology of the arts is partly the psychology of status has been repeatedly pointed out, not just by cynics and barbarians but by erudite social commentators such as Quentin Bell and Tom Wolfe.[3] But in the modern university, it is unmentioned, indeed, unmentionable. Academics and intellectuals are culture vultures. In a gathering of today's elite, it is perfectly acceptable to laugh that you barely passed Physics for Poets and Rocks for Jocks and have remained ignorant of science ever since, despite the obvious importance of scientific literacy to informed choices about personal health and public policy. But saying that you have never heard of James Joyce or that you tried listening to Mozart once but prefer Andrew Lloyd Webber is as shocking as blowing your nose on your sleeve or announcing that you employ children in your sweatshop, despite the obvious *un*importance of your tastes in leisure-time activity to just about anything. The blending in people's minds of art, status and virtue is an extension of Bell's principle of sartorial morality: people find dignity in the signs of an honourably futile existence removed from all menial necessities.

I mention these facts not to denigrate the arts but to clarify my topic. I want you to look at the psychology of the arts with the disinterested eye of an alien biologist trying to make sense of the human species rather than as a member of the species with a stake in how the arts are portrayed. *Of course* we find pleasure and enlightenment in contemplating the products of the arts, and not all of it is a pride in sharing the tastes of the beautiful people. But to understand the psychology of the arts that remains when we subtract out the psychology of status, we must leave at the door our terror of being mistaken for the kind of person who prefers Andrew Lloyd Webber to Mozart. We need to begin with folk songs, pulp fiction and paintings on black velvet, not Mahler, Eliot and Kandinsky. And that does *not* mean compensating for our slumming by dressing up the lowly subject matter in highfalutin 'theory' (a semiotic analysis of *Peanuts*, a psychoanalytic exegesis of Archie Bunker, a deconstruction of *Vogue*). It means asking a simple question: What is it about the mind that lets people take pleasure in shapes and colours and sounds and jokes and stories and myths?

That question might be answerable, whereas questions about art in general are not. Theories of art carry the seeds of their own destruction. In an age when any Joe can buy CDs, paintings and novels, artists make their careers by finding ways to avoid the hackneyed, to challenge jaded tastes, to differentiate the cognoscenti from the dilettantes, and to flout the current wisdom about what art is (hence the fruitless attempts over the decades to define art). Any discussion that fails to recognize that dynamic is doomed to sterility. It can never explain why music pleases the ear, because 'music' will be defined to encompass atonal jazz, chromatic compositions, and other intellectual exercises. It will never understand the bawdy laughs and convivial banter that are so important in people's lives because it will define humour as the arch wit of an Oscar Wilde. Excellence and the avant-garde are designed for the sophisticated palate, a product of years of immersion in a genre and a familiarity with its conventions and clichés. They rely on one-upmanship and allusions and displays of virtuosity. However fascinating and worthy of our support they are, they tend to obscure the psychology of aesthetics, not to illuminate it.

Another reason the psychology of the arts is obscure is that they are not adaptive in the biologist's sense of the word. In *How the Mind Works* I argued that the major components of the mind serve an adaptive function, but that does not mean that I believe that everything the mind does is biologically adaptive. The mind is a neural computer, fitted by natural selection with combinatorial algorithms for causal and probabilistic reasoning about plants, animals, objects and people. It is driven by goal states that served biological fitness in ancestral environments, such as food, sex, safety, parenthood, friendship, status and knowledge. That toolbox, however, can be used to assemble Sunday afternoon projects of dubious adaptive value.

Some parts of the mind register the attainment of increments of fitness by giving us a sensation of pleasure. Other parts use a knowledge of cause and effect to bring about goals. Put them together and you get a mind that rises to a biologically pointless challenge: figuring out how to get at the pleasure circuits of the brain and deliver little jolts of enjoyment without the inconvenience of wringing bona fide fitness increments from the harsh world. When a rat has access to a lever that sends electrical impulses to an electrode implanted in its medial forebrain bundle, it presses the lever furiously until it drops of exhaustion, forgoing opportunities to eat, drink and have sex. People don't yet undergo elective neurosurgery to have electrodes implanted in their pleasure centres, but they have found ways to stimulate them by other means. An obvious example is recreational drugs, which seep into the chemical junctions of the pleasure circuits.

Another route to the pleasure circuits is via the senses, which stimulate the circuits when they are in environments that would have led to fitness in past generations. Of course a fitness-promoting environment cannot announce itself directly. It gives off patterns of sounds, sights, smells, tastes, and feels that the senses are designed to register. Now, if the intellectual faculties could identify the pleasure-giving patterns, purify them, and concentrate them, the brain could stimulate itself without the messiness of electrodes or drugs. It could give itself intense artificial doses of the sights and sounds and smells that ordinarily are given off by healthful environments. We enjoy strawberry cheesecake, but not because we evolved a taste for it. We evolved circuits that gave us trickles of enjoyment from the sweet taste of ripe fruit, the creamy feel of fats and oils from nuts and meat, and the coolness of fresh water. Cheesecake packs a sensual wallop unlike anything in the natural world because it is a brew of mega-doses of agreeable stimuli which we concocted for the express purpose of pressing our pleasure buttons. Pornography is another pleasure technology. The arts are a third.

There is another way that the design of the mind can throw off fascinating but biologically functionless activities. The intellect evolved to crack the defences of things in the natural and social world. It is made up of modules for reasoning about how objects, artefacts, living things, animals, and other human minds work.[4] There are problems in the universe other than those: where the universe came from, how physical flesh can give rise to sentient minds, why bad things happen to good people, what happens to our thoughts and feelings when we die. The mind can pose such questions but may not be equipped to answer them, even if the questions have answers. Given that the mind is a product of natural selection, it should not have a miraculous ability to commune with all truths; it should have a mere ability to solve problems that are sufficiently similar to the mundane survival challenges of ancestors. According to a saying, if you give a boy a hammer, the whole world becomes a nail. If you give a species an elementary grasp of mechanics, biology and psychology, the whole world becomes a machine, a jungle and a society. I will suggest that religion and philosophy are in part the application of mental tools to problems they were not designed to solve.

Some readers may be surprised to learn that after spending the better part of a book (*How the Mind Works*) reverse-engineering the major parts of the mind, I can argue that some of the activities we consider most profound are non-adaptive by-products. But both kinds of argument come from a single standard, the criteria for biological adaptation. For the same reason that it is wrong to write off - language, stereo vision and the emotions as evolutionary accidents – namely, their universal, complex, reliably developing, well-engineered, reproduction-promoting design – it is wrong to invent functions for activities that lack that design merely because we want to ennoble them with the imprimatur of biological adaptiveness. Many writers have said that the 'function' of the arts is to bring the community together, to help us see the world in new ways, to give us a sense of harmony with the cosmos, to allow us to experience the sublime, and so on. All these claims are true, but none is about adaptation in the technical sense of a mechanism that brings about effects that would have increased the number of copies of the genes building that mechanism in the environment in which we evolved. Some aspects of the arts, I think, do have functions in this sense, but most do not.

*   *   *

'The fact is I am quite happy in a movie, even a bad movie. Other people, so I have read, treasure memorable moments in their lives.' At least the narrator of Walker Percy's novel *The Moviegoer* acknowledges the difference. Television stations get mail from soap-opera viewers with death threats for the evil characters, advice to the lovelorn ones, and booties for the babies. Mexican moviegoers have been known to riddle the screen with bullets. Actors complain that fans confuse them with their roles; Leonard Nimoy wrote a memoir called *I Am Not Spock*, then gave up and wrote another one called *I Am Spock*. These anecdotes appear regularly in the newspapers, usually to insinuate that people today are boobs who cannot distinguish fantasy from reality.

I suspect that the people are not literally deluded but are going to extremes to enhance the pleasure we all get from losing ourselves in fiction. Where does this motive, found in all peoples, come from?

Horace wrote that the purpose of literature is 'to delight and instruct',[5] a function echoed centuries later by John Dryden when he defined a play as 'a just and lively image of human nature, representing its passions and humours, and the changes of fortune to which it is subject; for the delight and instruction of mankind'.[6] It's helpful to distinguish the delight, perhaps the product of a useless technology for pressing our pleasure buttons, from the instruction, perhaps a product of a cognitive adaptation.

The technology of fiction delivers a simulation of life that an audience can enter in the comfort of their cave, couch or theatre seat. Words can evoke mental images, which can activate the parts of the brain that register the world when we actually perceive it. Other technologies violate the assumptions of our perceptual apparatus and trick us with illusions that partly duplicate the experience of seeing and hearing real events. They include costumes, makeup, sets, sound effects, cinematography and animation. Perhaps in the near future we can add virtual reality to the list, and in the more distant future the feelies of *Brave New World*.

When the illusions work, there is no mystery to the question 'Why do people enjoy fiction?' It is identical to the question 'Why do people enjoy life?' When we are absorbed in a book or a movie, we get to see breathtaking landscapes, hobnob with important people, fall in love with ravishing men and women, protect loved ones, attain impossible goals, and defeat wicked enemies. Not a bad deal for seven dollars and 50 cents!

Of course, not all stories have happy endings. Why would we pay seven dollars and 50 cents for a simulation of life that makes us miserable? Sometimes, as with art films, it is to gain status through cultural machismo. We endure a pummelling of the emotions to differentiate ourselves from the crass philistines who actually go to the movies to enjoy themselves. Sometimes it is the price we pay to satisfy two incompatible desires: stories with happy endings and stories with unpredictable endings, which preserve the illusion of a real world. There have to be some stories in which the murderer does catch up with the heroine in the basement, or we would never feel suspense and relief in the stories in which she escapes. The economist Steven Landsburg observes that happy endings predominate when no director is willing to sacrifice the popularity of his or her film for the greater good of more suspense in the movies in general.[7]

But then how can we explain the tearjerker, aimed at a market of moviegoers who *enjoy* being defrauded into grief? The psychologist Paul Rozin lumps tearjerkers with other examples of benign masochism like smoking, riding on roller coasters, eating hot chilli peppers, and sitting in saunas.[8] Benign masochism is like the drive of Tom Wolfe's test pilots to push the outside of the envelope. It expands the range of options in life by testing, in small increments, how closely one can approach a brink of disaster without falling over it. Of course the theory would be vacuous if it offered a glib explanation for every inexplicable act, and it would be false if it predicted that people would pay to have needles stuck under their fingernails. But the idea is more subtle. Benign masochists must be confident that no serious harm will befall them. They must bring on the pain or fear in measured increments. And they must have an opportunity to control and mitigate the damage. The technology of tearjerkers seems to fit. Moviegoers know the whole time that when they leave the theatre they will find their loved ones unharmed. The heroine is done in by a progressive disease, not a heart attack or a piece of hot dog stuck in the throat, so we can prepare our emotions for the tragedy. We only have to accept the abstract premise that the heroine will die; we are excused from watching the disagreeable details. (Greta Garbo, Ali MacGraw, and Debra Winger all looked quite lovely as they wasted away from consumption and cancer.) And the viewer must identify with the next of kin, empathize with their struggle to cope, and feel confident that life will go on. Tearjerkers simulate a triumph over tragedy.

Even following the foibles of ordinary virtual people as they live their lives can press a pleasure button, the one labelled 'gossip'. Gossip is a favourite pastime in all human societies because knowledge is power. Knowing who needs a favour and who is in a position to offer one, who is trustworthy and who is a liar, who is available (or soon to become available) and who is under the protection of a jealous spouse or family – all give obvious strategic advantages in the games of life. That is especially true when the information is not yet widely known and one can be the first to exploit an opportunity, the social equivalent of insider trading. In the small bands in which our minds evolved, everyone knew everyone else, so all gossip was useful. Today, when we peer into the private lives of fictitious characters, we are giving ourselves the same buzz.

Literature, though, not only delights but instructs. The computer scientist Jerry Hobbs has tried to reverse-engineer the fictional narrative in an essay he was tempted to call 'Will Robots Ever Have Literature?'[9] Novels, he concluded, work like experiments. The author places a fictitious character in a hypothetical situation in an otherwise real world where ordinary facts and laws hold, and allows the reader to explore the consequences. We can imagine that there was a person in Dublin named Leopold Bloom with the personality, family and occupation that James Joyce attributed to him, but we would object if we were suddenly to learn that the British sovereign at the time was not King Edward but Queen Edwina. Even in science fiction, we are asked to suspend belief in a few laws of physics, say to get the heroes to the next galaxy, but the events should otherwise unfold according to lawful causes and effects. A surreal story like Kafka's *Metamorphosis* begins with one counterfactual premise – a man can turn into an insect – and plays out the consequences in a world where everything else is the same. The hero retains his human consciousness, and we follow him as he makes his way and people react to him as real people would react to a giant insect. Only in fiction that is *about* logic and reality, such as *Alice's Adventures in Wonderland*, can any strange thing happen.

Once the fictitious world is set up, the protagonist is given a goal and we watch as he or she pursues it in the face of obstacles. It is no coincidence that this standard definition of plot is identical to the definition of intelligence I suggested in *How the Mind Works*, namely, the ability to attain goals in the face of obstacles by means of decisions based on rational (truth-obeying) rules. Characters in a fictitious world do exactly what our intelligence allows us to do in the real world.[10] We watch what happens to them and mentally take note of the outcomes of the strategies and tactics they use in pursuing their goals.

What are those goals? A Darwinian would say that ultimately organisms have only two: to survive and to reproduce. And those are precisely the goals that drive the human organisms in fiction. There are a small number of plots in the world's fiction and drama, and the scholar Georges Polti claims to have listed them all.[11] Most of the 36 plots in his catalogue are defined by love or sex or a threat to the safety of the protagonist or his kin (for example, 'Mistaken jealousy', 'Vengeance taken for kindred upon kindred', and 'Discovery of the dishonour of a loved one'). The difference between fiction for children and fiction for adults is commonly summed up in two words: sex and violence. Woody Allen's homage to Russian literature was entitled *Love and Death*. Pauline Kael got the title for one of her books of movie criticism from an Italian movie poster that she said contained 'the briefest statement imaginable of the basic appeal of the movies': *Kiss Kiss Bang Bang*.[12]

Sex and violence are not just the obsessions of pulp fiction and trash TV. The language maven Richard Lederer and the computer programmer Michael Gilleland present the following tabloid headlines:

CHICAGO CHAUFFEUR SMOTHERS BOSS'S DAUGHTER, THEN CUTS HER UP AND STUFFS HER IN FURNACE

DOCTOR'S WIFE AND LOCAL MINISTER EXPOSED FOR CONCEIVING ILLEGITIMATE DAUGHTER

TEENAGERS COMMIT DOUBLE SUICIDE; FAMILIES VOW TO END VENDETTA

STUDENT CONFESSES TO AXE MURDER OF LOCAL PAWNBROKER AND ASSISTANT

GARAGE OWNER STALKS AFFLUENT BUSINESSMAN, THEN SHOTGUNS HIM IN HIS SWIMMING POOL

MADWOMAN LONG IMPRISONED IN ATTIC SETS HOUSE ON FIRE, THEN LEAPS TO DEATH

FORMER SCHOOLTEACHER, FOUND TO HAVE BEEN PROSTITUTE, COMMITTED TO INSANE ASYLUM

PRINCE ACQUITTED OF KILLING MOTHER IN REVENGE FOR MURDER OF HIS FATHER

Sound familiar?[13]

Fiction is especially compelling when the obstacles to the protagonist's goals are other people in pursuit of incompatible goals. Life is like chess, and plots are like those books of famous chess games that serious players study so they will be prepared if they ever find themselves in similar straits. The books are handy because chess is combinatorial; at any stage there are too many possible sequences of moves and countermoves for them all to be played out in one's mind. General strategies like 'get your queen out early' are too vague to be of much use, given the trillions of situations the rules permit. A good training regime is to build up a mental catalogue of tens of thousands of game challenges and the moves that allowed good players to do well in them. In artificial intelligence, it is called case-based reasoning.

Life has even more moves than chess. People are always, to some extent, in conflict, and their moves and countermoves multiply out to an unimaginably vast set of interactions. Partners, like the prisoners in the hypothetical dilemma, can either cooperate or defect, on this move and on subsequent moves. Parents, offspring and siblings, because of their partial genetic overlap, have both common and competing interests, and any deed that one party directs toward another may be selfless, selfish, or a mixture of the two. When boy meets girl, either or both may see the other as a spouse, as a one-night stand, or neither. Spouses may be faithful or adulterous. Friends may be false friends.

Allies may assume less than their fair share of the risk, or may defect as the finger of fate turns toward them. Strangers may be competitors or outright enemies. These games are taken into higher dimensions by the possibility of deception, which allows words and deeds to be either true or false, and self-deception, which allows *sincere* words and deeds to be either true or false. They are expanded into still higher dimensions by rounds of paradoxical tactics and countertactics, in which a person's usual goals – control, reason and knowledge – are voluntarily surrendered to make the person unthreatenable, trustworthy, or too dangerous to challenge.

The intrigues of people in conflict can multiply out in so many ways that no one could possibly play out the consequences of all courses of action in the mind's eye. Fictional narratives supply us with a mental catalogue of the fatal conundrums we might face someday and the outcomes of strategies we could deploy in them. What are the options if I were to suspect that my uncle killed my father, took his position, and married my mother? If my hapless older brother got no respect in the family, are there circumstances that might lead him to betray me? What's the worst that could happen if I were seduced by a client while my wife and daughter were away for the weekend? What's the worst that could happen if I had an affair to spice up my boring life as the wife of a country doctor? How can I avoid a suicidal confrontation with raiders who want my land today without looking like a coward and thereby ceding it to them tomorrow? The answers are to be found in any bookstore or video shop. The cliché that life imitates art is true because the function of some kinds of art is for life to imitate it.

Notes

1. This chapter is adapted from Steven Pinker, *How the Mind Works* (New York: Norton, 1997; London: Penguin Books, 1998), pp. 521–6, 538–43, and is reproduced by kind permission of W. W. Norton & Company, Inc. and Penguin Books Ltd.

2. Thorstein Veblen, *The Theory of the Leisure Class* (1899; repr. New York: Penguin, 1994); Quentin Bell, *On Human Finery* (1947; repr. London: Allison & Busby, 1992).

3. See Bell, *On Human Finery*; Tom Wolfe, *The Painted Word* (New York: Bantam Books, 1975).

4. See *How the Mind Works*, Chapter 5.

5. Quoted by Jerry R. Hobbs, *Literature and Cognition* (Stanford, CA: Center for the Study of Language and Information, 1990), p. 5.

6. Quoted by Joseph Carroll, *Evolution and Literary Theory* (Columbia, MO: University of Missouri Press, 1995), p. 170.

7. Steven E. Landsburg, *The Armchair Economist: Economics and Everyday Life* (New York: Free Press, 1993).

8. Paul Rozin, 'Towards a Psychology of Food and Eating', *Current Directions in Psychological Science*, 5 (1996), pp. 18–24.

9. Hobbs, *Literature and Cognition*. See also Mark Turner, *Reading Minds: The Study of English in an Age of Cognitive Science* (Princeton, NJ: Princeton University Press, 1991).

10. See Carroll, *Evolution and Literary Theory*.

11. Georges Polti, *The Thirty-Six Dramatic Situations*, trans. L. Ray (1921; repr. Boston: The Writer, Inc., 1977).

12. Pauline Kael, *Kiss Kiss Bang Bang* (Boston: Little, Brown, 1968), prefatory 'Note on the Title'.

13. Tabloid headlines: *Native Son* by Richard Wright; *The Scarlet Letter* by Nathaniel Hawthorne; *Romeo and Juliet* by William Shakespeare; *Crime and Punishment* by Fyodor Dostoevsky; *The Great Gatsby* by F. Scott Fitzgerald; *Jane Eyre* by Charlotte Brontë; *A Streetcar Named Desire* by Tennessee Williams; *Eumenides* by Aeschylus. All from Richard Lederer and Michael Gilleland, *Literary Trivia: Fun and Games for Book Lovers* (New York: Vintage, 1994).

2 Literature, science and human nature

Ian McEwan

Greatness in literature is more intelligible and amenable to most of us than greatness in science. All of us have an idea, our own or one that has been imposed upon us, of what is meant by a great novelist. Whether it is in a spirit of awe and delight, duty or scepticism, we grasp at first hand, when we read *Anna Karenina*, or *Madame Bovary*, what people mean when they speak of greatness. We have the privilege of unmediated contact. From the first sentence, we come into a presence, and we can see for ourselves the quality of a particular mind; in a matter of minutes we may read the fruits of a long-forgotten afternoon, an afternoon's work done in isolation, 150 years ago. And what was once an unfolding personal secret, is now ours. Imaginary people appear before us, their historical and domestic circumstances are very particular, their characters equally so. We witness and judge the skill with which they are conjured. By an unspoken agreement, a kind of contract between writer and reader, it is assumed that however strange these people are, we will understand them readily enough to be able to appreciate their strangeness. To do this, we must bring our own general understanding of what it means to be a person. We have, in the terms of cognitive psychology, a theory of mind, a more or less automatic understanding of what it means to be someone else. Without this understanding, as the psychopathology shows, we would find it virtually impossible to form and sustain relationships, read expressions or intentions, or perceive how we ourselves are understood. To the particular instances that are presented to us in a novel, we bring this deep and broad understanding.

When Saul Bellow's Herzog stands in front of a mirror – as characters in fiction so often and conveniently do – he is wearing only a newly purchased straw hat and underpants. His mother

> wanted [him] to become a rabbi and he seemed to himself gruesomely unlike a rabbi now in the trunks and straw hat, his face charged with heavy

sadness, foolish utter longing of which a religious life might have purged him. That mouth! – heavy with desire and irreconcilable anger, the straight nose sometimes grim, the dark eyes! And his figure! – the long veins winding in the arms and filling in the hanging hands, an ancient system, of greater antiquity than the Jews themselves . . . Bare legged, he looked like a Hindu.[1]

A reader may not understand from the inside every specific of Herzog's condition – a mid-twentieth-century American, a Jew, a city dweller, a divorcee, an alienated intellectual, and nor might a young reader sympathize with the remorse of early middle age, but self-scrutiny that is edging towards a reckoning has a general currency, as does the droll, *faux-naïve* perception that one's biology – the circulatory system – predates, and by implication, is even more of the essence of being human, than one's religion. Literature flourishes along the channels of this unspoken agreement between writers and readers, offering a mental map whose north and south are the specific, and the general. At its best, literature is universal, illuminating human nature at precisely the point at which it is most parochial and specific.

Greatness in science is harder for most of us to grasp. We can make a list of scientists we have been told are great, but few of us have had the kind of intimate contact that would illuminate the particular qualities of the achievement. Partly, it is the work itself – it does not invite us in – its objectifying, therefore distancing, corrupted by difficult or seemingly irrelevant detail. Mathematics is also a barrier. Furthermore, scientific ideas happily float free of their creators. Scientists might know the classical Laws of Motion but have never read Newton on the matter, or have grasped relativity from text books without reading Einstein's Special or General Theories, or know the structure of DNA without having – or needing – a first-hand knowledge of Crick and Watson's 1953 paper. Here is a good case in point. Their paper, a mere twelve hundred words, published in the journal *Nature*, ended with the famously modest conclusion: 'It has not escaped our notice that the specific pairing we have postulated immediately suggests a possible copying mechanism for the genetic material.'[2] 'It has not escaped our notice . . .' – the drawing room politesse of the double negative is touchingly transparent. It roughly translates as 'Look at us everybody! We've found the mechanism by which life on earth replicates, we're excited as hell and can't sleep a wink . . .' 'It has not escaped our notice' is the kind of close contact I mean. It is not easily come by at first hand.

However, there is one pre-eminent scientist who is almost as approachable in this respect as a novelist. It is perfectly possible for the non-scientist to understand what it is in Darwin's work which makes him unique and great. In part, it is the sequence of benign accidents that set him on his course, each step to be measured against the final achievement. And partly it is the subject itself. Natural history, or biology generally, is a descriptive science. The theory of natural selection is not, in its essentials, difficult to understand, though its implications have been vast, its applications formidable and the consequences in scientific terms quite complex – as the computational biology of the late Bill Hamilton shows. Partly too, because Darwin, though hardly the greatest prose writer of the nineteenth century, was intensely communicative, affectionate, intimate and honest. He wrote many letters, and filled many notebooks.

Let us read his life as a novel, like *Herzog*, driving forwards towards a great reckoning. The 16-year-old Charles is at the University in Edinburgh and beginning to show disillusionment with the study of medicine. He writes to his sisters that 'I am going to learn to stuff birds, from a blackamoor.'[3] Charles took his lessons in taxidermy from one John Edmonstone, a freed slave, and found his teacher 'very pleasant and intelligent'. Edmonstone recounted to the young Darwin his experiences as a slave, and described the wonders of a tropical rain forest to him. All his life, Darwin abhorred slavery, and this early acquaintanceship may have had some bearing on the relatively neglected book of Darwin's I want to discuss. The following year Darwin comes in contact with the evolutionary ideas of Lamarck, and in the Edinburgh debating societies hears passionate, godless arguments for scientific materialism. He spends days foraging along the shores of the Firth of Forth looking for sea creatures and an 1827 notebook records detailed observations of two marine invertebrates.

Since Charles does not warm to the prospect of becoming a physician, his father 'proposed that I should become a clergyman. He was very properly vehement against my turning an idle sporting man, which then seemed my probable destination.'[4] So he studies at Cambridge where at the age of eighteen, his love of natural history is becoming a passion. 'What fun we will have together,' he writes to his cousin, 'what beetles we will catch, it will do my heart good to go once more together to some of our old haunts . . . we will make regular campaigns into the Fens; Heaven protect the beetles.'[5] And in another letter, 'I am dying by inches from not having anybody to talk to about insects.'[6] In his last two terms, his mentor, Henslowe, Professor of Botany, persuades him to take up geology.

After Cambridge, the offer comes through Henslowe to be the naturalist and companion to the captain on board the *Beagle* making a government survey of South America. We may follow the wrangling as he persuades his father, with the help of Uncle Joseph Wedgwood. 'I must state again', implores the earnest Charles, 'I cannot think it would unfit me hereafter for a steady life.'[7] Many weeks of delay; then after two false starts, he sets sail on 27 December 1831. Days of seasickness, then the *Beagle* is prevented by quarantine measures from landing in La Palma in the Canaries. But Charles has a net in the stern of the ship, the weather is fine and he catches 'a great number of curious animals, and fully occupied my time in my cabin'.[8] Finally, landfall at St Jago in the Cape de Verde islands, and the young man is in ecstasy. 'The island has given me so much instruction and delight . . .' he writes to his father,

it is utterly useless to say anything about the scenery – it would be as profitable to explain to a blind man colours, as to a person who has not been out of Europe, the total dissimilarity of a tropical view . . . Whenever I enjoy anything I always look forward to writing it down . . . So you must excuse raptures and those raptures badly expressed.[9]

He enjoys working in his cramped cabin, drawing and describing his specimens of rocks, plants and animals and preserving them to send back to England, to Henslowe. The enthusiasm does not die as the expedition proceeds, but to it is added a growing scientific confidence. He writes to Henslowe,

> nothing has so much interested me as finding two species of elegantly coloured Planariae, inhabiting the dry forest! The false relation they bear to snails is the most extraordinary thing of the kind I have ever seen . . . some of the marine species possess an organization so marvellous that I can scarcely credit my eyesight . . . Today I have been out and returned like Noah's ark, with animals of all sorts . . . I have found a most curious snail, and spiders, beetles, snakes, scorpions ad libitum. And to conclude, shot a Cavia weighing one hundredweight . . .'[10]

With vast quantities of his preserved specimens preceding him, and already being described, and with his own theories about the formation of the earth, and of coral reefs, taking shape in his mind, Darwin arrives back in England five years later, at the age of 27, already a scientist of some standing. There is something of the thrill and illumination of great literature when Darwin, at the age of 29, only two years after he has returned from his voyage on the *Beagle*, and still 21 years before he will publish *The Origin of Species*, confides to a pocket notebook the first hints of a simple, beautiful idea: 'Origin of man now proved . . . He who understands baboon would do more towards metaphysics than Locke.'[11]

And yet *The Origin of Species* itself does not allow an easy route into an understanding of Darwin's greatness. Read as a book rather than as a theory, it can overwhelm the non-specialist reader with a proliferation of instances – the fruits of Darwin's delay – and it is significant that the most frequently quoted passages occur in the final paragraph.

Darwin was the sort of scientist whose work completely permeated his life. His study of the earthworms in the garden at Downe is well known. He attended country markets to quiz horse, dog and pig breeders, and at country shows he sought out growers of prize vegetables. 'My first child was born on December 27th 1839, and I at once commenced to make notes on the first dawn of the various expressions which he exhibited . . .'[12] Long before an innate theory of mind had been postulated, Darwin was experimenting and reaching his own conclusions:

> When a few days over six months old, his nurse pretended to cry, and I saw that his face instantly assumed a melancholy expression, with the corners of the mouth strongly depressed. Therefore it seems to me that an innate feeling must have told him that the pretended crying of his nurse expressed grief; and this, through the instinct of sympathy, excited grief in him.[13]

While out riding, he stops to talk to a woman, and notes the contraction in her brows as she looks up at him with the sun at his back. At home he takes three of his children out into the garden and gets them to look up at a bright portion of the sky. The reason? 'With all three, the orbicular, corrugator, and pyramidal muscles were energetically contracted, through reflex action . . .'[14] Over many years, while engaged on other work, Darwin was researching the *Expression of the Emotions in Man and Animals*, his most extraordinary and approachable book, rich in observed detail and brilliant speculation, beautifully illustrated – one of the first scientific books to use photographs, including some of his own baby pouting and laughing – and now available in a third edition, prepared and annotated by the great American psychologist of the emotions, Paul Ekman.

Darwin not only sets out to describe expressions in dogs and cats as well as man – how we contract the muscles around our eyes when we are angry and reveal our canine teeth, and how, in Ekman's words, we want to touch with our faces those we love – he also poses the difficult question why.[15] Why do we redden with embarrassment rather than go pale? Why do the inner corners of the brow lift in sorrow, and not the whole brow? Why do cats arch their backs in affection? An emotion, he argues, is a physiological state, a direct expression of physiological change. In pursuit of these questions, there are numerous pleasing digressions and observations: the way a billiard player, especially a novice, tries to guide the ball towards its target with a movement of the head, or even the whole body. How a cross child sitting on its parent's knee raises one shoulder and gives a backward push with it in an expression of rejection; the firm closure of the mouth during a delicate or difficult operation.

Behind this wealth of detail lay more basic questions. Do we *learn* to smile when we are happy, or is the smile innate? In other words, are expressions universal to all cultures and races, or are they culture specific? Darwin wrote to people in remote corners of the British Empire asking them to observe the expressions of the indigenous populations. In England he showed photographs of various expressions and asked people to comment on them. He drew on his own experience. The book is anecdotal, unscientific, and very clear-sighted. The expressions of emotion are the products of evolution, Darwin argued, and therefore universal. He opposed the influential views of the anatomist Sir Charles Bell that certain unique muscles, with no equivalent in the animal kingdom, had been created by God in the faces of men to allow them to communicate their feelings to each other. In a footnote, Ekman quotes from Bell's book: 'the most remarkable muscle in the human face is the corrugator supercilii which knits the eyebrows with an enigmatic effect which unaccountably but irresistibly conveys the idea of mind'.[16] In Darwin's copy of Bell's book, Darwin has underlined the passage and written, 'I suspect he never dissected a monkey.'[17] Of course, these muscles, as Darwin showed, existed in other primates.

By showing that the same principles governing expression applied in primates and man, Darwin argued for continuity and gradation of species – important generally to his theory of evolution, and to disproving the Christian view that man was a special creation, set apart from all other animals. He was intent too on demonstrating through universality a common descent for all races of mankind. In this he opposed himself forcefully to the racist views of scientists like Agassiz, who argued that Africans were inferior to Europeans because they were descended from a different and inferior stock. In a letter to his second cousin, William Darwin Fox, Darwin mentioned how Agassiz had been maintaining the doctrine of 'several species' (i.e. of man) 'much, I daresay, to the comfort of slave-holding Southerns'.[18]

Modern palaeontology and molecular biology show Darwin to have been right, and Agassiz wrong: we are descended from a common stock of anatomically modern humans who migrated out of east Africa, perhaps as recently as 200,000 years ago, and spread around the world. Local differences in climate have produced variations in the species that are in many cases literally skin deep. We have fetishized these differences to rationalize conquest and subjugation. As Darwin puts it:

> all the chief expressions exhibited by man are the same throughout the world. This fact is interesting as it affords a new argument in favour of the several races being descended from a single parent stock, which must have been almost completely human in structure, and to a large extent, in mind, before the period at which the races diverged from each other.[19]

We should be clear about what is implied by the universal expressions of emotion. The eating of a snail or a piece of cheddar cheese may give rise to delight in one culture and disgust in another. But disgust, regardless of the cause, has a universal expression – in Darwin's words, 'The mouth is opened widely, with the upper lip strongly retracted, which wrinkles the side of the nose . . .'[20] The expression and the physiology are products of evolution. But emotions are also, of course, shaped by culture. Our ways of managing our emotions, our attitudes to them, the way we describe them, are learned and differ from culture to culture. Still, behind the notion of a commonly held stock of emotion lies that of a universal human nature. And until fairly recently, and for a good part of the twentieth century, this has been a reviled notion. Darwin's book was out of favour for a long time after his death. The climate of opinion has changed now, and Ekman's superb edition has been enthusiastically welcomed.

As must be clear by now, I think that the exercise of imagination and ingenuity as expressed in literature supports Darwin's view. It would not be possible to read and enjoy literature from a time remote from our own, or from a culture that was profoundly different from our own, unless we shared some common emotional ground, some deep reservoir of assumptions, with the writer. A scholarly annotated edition that clarifies matters of historical circumstance or local custom or language is always useful, but it is never fundamentally necessary to a reading. What we have in common with each other is just as extraordinary in its way as all our exotic differences. I mentioned at the beginning the parochial and the universal as polarities in literature. One might think of literature as encoding both our cultural and genetic inheritance. Each of these two elements, genes and culture, have had a reciprocal shaping effect, for as primates we are intensely social creatures, and our social environment has exerted over time a powerful adaptive pressure. This gene-culture co-evolution, elaborated by E. O. Wilson among others, dissolves the oppositions of nature versus nurture. If one reads accounts of the systematic non-intrusive observations of troupes of bonobo – bonobos and chimps rather than baboons are our closest relatives – one sees rehearsed all the major themes of the English nineteenth-century novel: alliances made and broken, individuals rising while others fall, plots hatched, revenge, gratitude, injured pride, successful and unsuccessful courtship, bereavement and mourning. Approximately five million years separate us and the bonobos from our common ancestor – and given that a lot of this coming and going is ultimately about sex (I'm talking here about bonobos *and* the nineteenth-century novel) that is a very long time during which, cumulatively, successful social strategies effect the distribution of certain genes and not others.

That we have a nature, that its values are self-evident to us to the point of invisibility, and that it would be a different nature if we were, say, termites, was a point Wilson was trying to make when he invented a highly educated, professorial termite, the Dean of Termities, who delivers a stirring commencement-day address to his fellow termites:

> Since our ancestors, the macrotermitine termites, achieved ten-kilogram weight and larger brains during their rapid evolution through the later Tertiary Period, and learned to write with pheromonal script, termitistic scholarship has elevated and refined ethical philosophy. It is now possible to express the imperatives of moral behavior with precision. These imperatives are mostly self-evident and universal. They are the very essence of termity. They include the love of darkness and of the deep saprophytic, basidiomycetic penetralia of the soil; the centrality of colony life amidst a richness of war and trade with other colonies; the sanctity

of the physiological caste system; the evil of personal rights (the colony is ALL!); our deep love for the royal siblings allowed to reproduce; the joy of chemical song; the aesthetic pleasure and deep social satisfaction of eating feces from nestmates' anuses after the shedding of our skins; and the ecstasy of cannibalism and surrender of our own bodies for consumption when sick or injured . . . Some termitistically inclined scientists, particularly the ethologists and sociobiologists, argue that our social organisation is shaped by our genes and that our ethical precepts simply reflect the peculiarities of termite evolution. They assert that ethical philosophy must take into account the structure of the termite brain and the evolutionary history of the species. Socialisation is genetically channelled and some forms of it all but inevitable. This proposal has created major academic controversy . . .[21]

That is to say that whether it is a saga, a concrete poem, a *Bildungsroman* or a haiku, and regardless of when it was written and in what colony, you would just *know* a piece of termite literature as soon as you would read a line or two. Extrapolating from the termite literary tradition, we can say that our own human literature does not define human nature so much as exemplify it.

If there are human universals that transcend culture, then it follows that they do not change, or they do not change easily. And if something does change in us historically, then by definition, it is not human nature that has changed, but some characteristic special to a certain time and circumstance. And yet there are writers who like to make their point by assuming that human nature is a frail entity, subject to sudden lurches – exciting revolutionary improvements or deeply regrettable deterioration. Defining the moment of choice has always been an irresistible intellectual pursuit. No one, I think, has yet exceeded Virginia Woolf for precision in this matter, though she does allow a certain ironic haziness about the actual date: 'On or about December 1910', she wrote in her essay 'Character in Fiction', 'human character changed.'[22] Woolf of course was preoccupied with the great gulf, as she saw it, that separated her generation from her parents'. The famous anecdote may or may not be true, but one hopes it was. It has

Lytton Strachey entering a drawing room in 1908, encountering Virginia and her sister, pointing to a stain on Vanessa's dress and enquiring, 'Semen?' Virginia wrote, 'With that one word, all barriers of reticence and reserve went down.'[23] The nineteenth century had officially ended. The world would never be the same again.

I remember similar apocalyptic generational claims made in the 1960s and early 1970s. Human nature changed forever, it was claimed at the time, in a field near Woodstock in 1967, or in the same year with the release of *Sergeant Pepper*, or the year before on a certain undistinguished street in San Francisco. The Age of Aquarius had dawned, and things would never be the same again.

Less light-headed than Virginia Woolf but equally definitive, was T. S. Eliot in his essay 'The Metaphysical Poets'. He discovered that in the seventeenth century 'a dissociation of sensibility set in, from which we have never recovered'.[24] He was, of course, speaking of English poets, who 'possessed a mechanism of sensibility which could devour any kind of experience' but I think we can assume that he thought they generally shared a biology with other people. His theory, which, as he conceded, was perhaps too brief to carry conviction, expressed both Eliot's regret (this dissociation was not a good thing) and his hopes (this dissociation could be reversed by those modern poets who would redefine modern sensibilities to his prescription).

Jacob Burckhardt, defining his own choice moment, in *The Civilization of the Renaissance in Italy*, discerned a blossoming, not simply in human nature, but in consciousness itself: 'In the Middle Ages', he wrote,

> both sides of human consciousness – that which was turned within as that which was turned without – lay dreaming or half-awake beneath a common veil. Man was conscious of himself only as a member of a race, people, party, family, or corporation . . . But at the close of the thirteenth century, Italy began to swarm with individuality; the ban laid upon human personality was dissolved . . .'[25]

The French historian Philippe Ariès defined a radical shift in human emotions in the eighteenth century when parents began to feel a self-conscious love for their children. Before then, a child was little more than a tiny, incapable adult, likely to be carried off by disease and therefore not worth investing with too much feeling.[26] A thousand medieval tombstones and their heartfelt inscriptions to a departed child may have provided the graveyard for this particular theory, but Ariès' work demonstrates a secondary or parallel ambition in the pursuit of the defining moment of change in human nature – that is, the aim of locating the roots of our modernity. This is more or less central to the project of intellectual history – to ask at which moment, in which set of circumstances, we became recognizable to ourselves. At least some of these candidates will be familiar to you: the invention of agriculture 10,000 years ago, or, perhaps closely related, the expulsion from the Garden of Eden. Or the writing of Hamlet – a man so anguished, bored, indecisive and generally put-upon by the fact of his own existence that we welcome him into our hearts and find no precursor for him in literature. We can fix the beginnings of the modern mind in the scientific revolution of the seventeenth century; the agricultural or industrial revolutions which gathered populations into cities, and eventually made possible mass consumption, mass political parties, mass communication; the writings of Kafka; the invention of writing itself, a mere several thousand years ago which made possible a geometrical increase in the transmission of culture; the publication of Einstein's Special and General Theories; the first performance of the *Rite of Spring*; the publication of Joyce's *Ulysses*; or the dropping of a nuclear weapon on Hiroshima after which we accepted, whether we wanted it or not, stewardship for the whole planet. Some used to plump for the storming of the Winter Palace, though I would prefer to that the radically unadorned, conversationally reflective early poetry of Wordsworth; or, by association, the French Enlightenment and the invention of universal human rights.

The biological view on the other hand is long, though no less interesting: one speaks not of a moment of change, but of an immeasurable tract of irretrievable time, whose traces are a handful of bones and stone artefacts which demand all our interpretative genius; with the neo-cortex evolving at the astonishing rate of an extra teaspoon of grey matter every hundred thousand years, hominids made tools, acquired language, became aware of their own existence and that of others, and of their mortality, took a view on the after-life, and accordingly buried their dead. Possibly the Neanderthals, who fell into extinction 30,000 years ago, were by these criteria the first into the modern age.

You could say that what is pursued in all these accounts is the secular equivalent of a creation myth. Literary writers seem to prefer an explosive, decisive moment, the miracle of a birth, to a dull continuum of infinitesimal change. More or less the whole time span of culture can be embraced when we ask: who is the oldest, who is the ur, modern human being – mitochondrial Eve, or Alan Turing?

Our interest in the roots of modernity is not just a consequence of accelerating social change; implicit in the idea of the definitive moment, of rupture with the past, is the notion that human nature is a specific historical product, shaped by shared values, circumstances of upbringing within a certain civilization – in other words, that there is no human nature at all beyond that which develops at a particular time and in a particular culture. By this view the mind is an all-purpose, infinitely adaptable computing machine operating a handful of wired-in rules. We are born *tabula rasa*, and it is our times that shape us.

This view, known to some as the Standard Social Science Model and to others as environmental determinism, was the dominant one in the twentieth century, particularly in its first half. It had its roots in anthropology, especially in the work of Margaret Mead and her followers, and in behavioural psychology. In *Sex and Temperament in Three Primitive Societies*, published in 1935, Mead wrote: 'We are forced to conclude that human nature is almost unbelievably malleable, responding accurately and contrastingly to contrasting cultural conditions.'[27] This view found endorsement across the social sciences, and solidified in the post-war years into a dogma that had clear political dimensions. There was a time when to challenge it with reference to a biological dimension to existence would be to court academic, and even social, pariah status. Like Christian theologians, the cultural determinists freed us from all biological constraints, and set mankind apart from all other life on earth. And within this view, the educated man or woman pronouncing on a favoured date for the transformation of human nature would be on firm ground epistemologically – we are what the world makes us, and when the world changes dramatically, then so do we in our essentials. It can all happen, as Virginia Woolf observed for herself, in the space of a generation.

The famous behaviourist John Watson, Professor of Psychology at Johns Hopkins University, published an influential book on child-rearing in 1928. As Christina Hardyment showed in her marvellous book *Dream Babies*, there is hardly a better window into the collective mind of a society, its view of human nature, than the childcare handbooks it produces:

> Give me a dozen healthy infants, [Watson wrote] well-formed, and my own specified world to bring them up in and I'll guarantee to take any one at random and train him to become any kind of specialist I might select – doctor, lawyer, merchant chief, and yes, even beggar-man and thief, regardless of his talents, penchants, tendencies, abilities, vocations, and race of his ancestors.[28]

Human nature was clay in his hands. I cannot help feeling that the following passage from Watson's childcare book, beyond its unintentional comedy, reflects or foretells a century of doomed, tragic social experiments in shaping human nature, and shows us a skewed science, devoid of evidence – and no less grotesque than the pseudo-science that perverted Darwin's work to promote theories of racial supremacy:

> The sensible way to bring up children is to treat them as young adults. Dress them, bathe them with care and circumspection. Let your behavior always be objective and kindly firm. Never hug and kiss them. Never let them sit in your lap. If you must, kiss them once on the forehead when they say goodnight. Shake hands with them in the morning. Give them a pat on the head when they make a good job of a difficult task . . . Put the child out in the back yard a large part of the time . . . Do this from the time

that it is born . . . Let it learn to overcome difficulties almost from the moment of birth . . . away from your watchful eye. If your heart is too tender, and you must watch the child, make yourself a peephole, so that you can see without being seen, or use a periscope.[29]

The Psychological Care of Infant and Child, hugely successful at the time, was pronounced by *Atlantic Monthly* to be 'a godsend to parents'.[30]

The ideas of Mead and Watson, who were simply prominent figures among many promoting the near infinite malleability of human nature, found general acceptance in the public, and in the universities, where their descendants flourish today in various forms, including the political correctness movement which holds that since the human condition is a social construct which in turn is defined by language, it is possible and desirable to reform the condition by changing the language. No one should doubt that some good impulses lay behind the Standard Model. Margaret Mead in particular, working at a time when the European empires had consolidated but had not yet begun to crumble, had a strong anti-racist element to her work, and she was determined to oppose the condescending view of primitive inferiority and to insist that each culture must be judged in its own terms. When Mead and Watson were at their most active, the Soviet revolution still held great hopes for mankind. If learning makes us what we are, then inequalities could be eliminated if we shared the same environment. Educate parents in the proper methods of childcare, and new generations of improved people would emerge. Human nature could be fundamentally remoulded by the makers of social policy. We were perfectible, and the wrongs and inequalities of the past could be rectified by radical alterations to the social environment. The cruelties and absurdities of Social Darwinism and eugenics, and later, the new threat posed by the social policies of Hitler's Germany, engendered a disgust with the biological perspective that helped entrench a belief in a socially determined nature that could be engineered for the better of all.

In fact, the Third Reich cast a long shadow over free scientific enquiry in the decades after the Second World War. Various branches of psychology were trapped by intellectual fear, deterred by recent history from considering the mind as a biological product of adaptive forces, even while, in nearby biology departments, from the 1940s onwards, Darwinism was uniting with Mendelian genetics and molecular biology to form the powerful alliance known as the Modern Synthesis.

In the late 1950s, the young Paul Ekman, who had no firm convictions of his own, set off for New Guinea with head-and-shoulder photographs of modern Americans expressing various emotions – surprise, fear, disgust, joy and so on. He discovered that his sample group of Stone Age Highlanders, who had had no, or virtually no, contact with the modern world, were able to make up easily recognizable stories about each expression. They also mimed for him the facial expressions in response to stories he gave them – you come across a pig that has been dead for some days. His work, and later, cleverly designed experiments with Japanese and Americans, which took into account the display rules of the different cultures, clearly vindicated Darwin's conclusions. As Ekman writes:

> Social experience influences attitudes about emotion, creates display and feeling rules, develops and tunes the particular occasions which will most rapidly call forth an emotion. The *expression* of our emotions, the particular configurations of muscular movements, however, appear to be fixed, enabling understanding across generations, across cultures, and within cultures between strangers as well as intimates.[31]

Before leaving for New Guinea Ekman had paid a visit to Margaret Mead. Her firm view was that facial expressions differ from culture to culture as much as customs and values. She was distinctly cool about Ekman's research. And yet, towards the end of her life, she explained in her autobiography in 1972 that she and her colleagues had held back from the consideration of the biological bases of behaviour because of anxieties about the political consequences. How strange, this reversal of historical circumstances, that for Mead universality in expression or in human nature should appear to lend support to racism, while for Darwin such considerations undermined its flimsy theoretical basis.

Mead and her generation of anthropologists, arriving at a Stone Age settlement with their notebooks, gifts and decent intentions, did not fully understand (though Darwin, along with most novelists could have told them) as they exchanged smiles and greetings with their subjects, what a vast pool of shared humanity, of shared assumptions, was necessary, and already being drawn on, for them to do their work. As the last of these precious cultures have vanished, the data have been revisited. Donald Brown, in his book *Human Universals*, compiled a list of what human individuals and societies hold in common.[32] It is both long, and, given the near infinite range of all possible patterns of behaviour, quite specific. When reading it, it is worth bearing in mind Wilson's termite dean. Brown includes – I'm choosing at random – tool making, preponderant right-handedness, specific childhood fears, knowledge that other people have an inner life, trade, giving of gifts, notions of justice, importance of gossip, hospitality, hierarchies, and so on. What's interesting about Brown's characterization of what he calls the Universal People, is the number of pages he devotes to language – again quite specific – for example, 'UP' language has contrasts between vowels and contrasts between stops and non-stops. Their language is symbolic, invariably contains nouns, verbs and the possessive. Extra proficiency in language invariably confers prestige. This surely, at the higher level of mental functioning, is what binds the human family. We know now that no blank-disk all-purpose machine could learn language at the speed and facility that a child does. A three-year-old daily solves scores of ill-posed problems. An instinct for language is a central part of our nature.

On our crowded planet, we are no longer able to visit Stone Age peoples untouched by modern times. Mead and her contemporaries would never have wanted to put the question, 'what is it that we hold in common with such people?' and anthropologists no longer have the opportunity of first contact. We can, however, reach to our bookshelves. Literature must be our anthropology. Here is a description – 2,700 years old – of a woman who has been waiting for more than two decades for her beloved husband to come home.

Someone has told her that he has at last arrived, and is down-stairs, and that she must go and greet him. But, she asks herself, is it really him?

> [She] started down from her lofty room, her heart
> in turmoil, torn . . . should she keep her distance,
> probe her husband? Or rush up to the man at once
> and kiss his head and cling to both his hands?
> As soon as she stepped over the stone threshold,
> slipping in, she took a seat at the closest wall
> and, radiant in the firelight, faced Odysseus now.
> There he sat, leaning against the great central column,
> eyes fixed on the ground, waiting, poised for whatever words
> his hardy wife might say when she caught sight of him.
> A long while she sat in silence . . . numbing wonder
> filled her heart as her eyes explored his face.
> One moment he seemed . . . Odysseus to the man, to the life –
> the next, no, he was not the man she knew,
> a huddled mass of rags was all she saw.[33]

So, still uncertain, Penelope tells Odysseus they will sleep in separate rooms, and she gives orders for the marriage bed to be moved out of the bedroom. But, of course, he knows this bed cannot be moved – he knocked it together himself, and reminds her just how he did it. Thus he proves beyond doubt he really is her husband; but now he is upset that she thought he was an imposter, and they are already heading for a marital spat:

> Penelope felt her knees go slack, her heart surrender,
> recognizing the strong clear signs that Odysseus offered.
> She dissolved in tears, rushed to Odysseus, flung her arms
> around his neck and kissed his head and cried out,
> 'Odysseus – don't flare up at me now, not you,
> always the most understanding man alive!
> The gods, it was the gods who sent us sorrow –
> they grudged us both a life in each other's arms

from the heady zest of youth to the stoop of old age.
But don't fault me, angry with me now because I failed,
at the first glimpse, to greet you, hold you, so . . .
In my heart of hearts I always cringed with fear
some fraud might come, beguile me with his talk.'[34]

Customs may change – dead suitors may be lying in the hallway, with no homicide charges pending. But we recognize the human essence of these lines. Within the emotional and the expressive we remain what we are. As Darwin put it in his conclusion to the *Expression*, 'the language of the emotions . . . is certainly of importance for the welfare of mankind'.[35] In Homer's case we extend Ekman's 'understanding across the generations' – a hundred and thirty of them at least.

*   *   *

The Human Genome Sequencing Consortium concluded its report in *Nature* with these words: 'Finally, it has not escaped our notice that the more we learn about the human genome, the more there is to explore.'[36] This form of respectful echoing within the tradition must surely appeal to those who admire literary modernism. And now that the human genome has been sequenced, it is reasonable to ask just whose genome was this anyway? What lucky individual was chosen to represent us all? Who is the universal person? The answer is that the genes of 15 people were merged into just the sort of composite, plausible, imaginary person a novelist might dream up, and here we contemplate the metaphorical convergence of these two noble and distinct forms of investigation into our condition: literature and science. That which binds us, our common nature, is what literature has always, knowingly and helplessly, given voice to. And it is this universality which science, now entering another of its exhilarating moments, is set to explore.

Notes

1. Saul Bellow, *Herzog* (Harmondsworth: Penguin, 1965), p. 28.
2. J. D. Watson and F. H. C. Crick, 'A Structure for Deoxyribose Nucleic Acid', *Nature*, 171 (2 April 1953), p. 737.
3. *The Correspondence of Charles Darwin* (1821–1866), ed. F. H. Burkhardt, S. Smith, *et al.*, 14 vols (Cambridge: Cambridge University Press, 1983–2004), Vol. 1, p. 29.
4. *The Autobiography of Charles Darwin, 1809–1882,* ed. N. Barlow (London: Collins, 1958), p. 56.
5. *The Correspondence of Charles Darwin,* Vol. 1, p. 101.
6. *The Correspondence of Charles Darwin,* Vol. 1, p. 56.
7. *The Correspondence of Charles Darwin,* Vol. 1, p. 133.
8. *The Correspondence of Charles Darwin,* Vol. 1, p. 202.
9. *The Correspondence of Charles Darwin,* Vol. 1, p. 202.
10. *The Correspondence of Charles Darwin,* Vol. 1, p. 247.
11. *Charles Darwin's Notebooks: 1836–1844: Geology, Transmutation of Species, Metaphysical Enquiries,* ed. Paul H. Barrett, Peter J. Jautrey, Sandra Herbert, David Kohn and Sydney Smith (Ithaca, NY: Cornell University Press, 1987), p. 539.
12. *The Autobiography of Charles Darwin, 1809–1882,* p. 131.
13. Charles Darwin, *The Expression of the Emotions in Man and Animals,* ed. Paul Ekman (Oxford: Oxford University Press, 1998), p. 354.
14. *The Expression of the Emotions,* p. 187.
15. Paul Ekman, Introduction to *The Expression of the Emotions,* p. xxi.
16. Ekman, Introduction to *The Expression of the Emotions,* p. xxv.
17. Ekman, Introduction to *The Expression of the Emotions,* p. xxv.
18. *The Correspondence of Charles Darwin,* Vol. 4, p. 353.
19. *The Expression of the Emotions,* p. 355.
20. *The Expression of the Emotions,* p. 256.
21. Edward O. Wilson, *In Search of Nature* (London: Allen Lane, 1997), p. 97.
22. Virginia Woolf, *Mr. Bennett and Mrs. Brown* (London: Hogarth Press, 1924), p. 4.

23. 'Old Bloomsbury', *Moments of Being: Unpublished Autobiographical Writings*, ed. Jeanne Schulkind (London: Chatto & Windus for Sussex University Press, 1976), p. 173.

24. 'The Metaphysical Poets', *Selected Essays*, 3rd edn (London: Faber & Faber, 1951), p. 288.

25. Jacob Burckhardt, *The Civilization of the Renaissance in Italy*, trans. S. G. C. Middleton, 2nd edn (Oxford and London: Phaidon, 1945), p. 81.

26. Philippe Ariès, *L'Enfant et la vie familiale sous l'Ancien régime* (Paris: Plon, 1960).

27. Margaret Mead, *Sex and Temperament in Three Primitive Societies* (London: Routledge & Kegan Paul, 1935), p. 280.

28. John B. Watson, *Behaviorism* (London: Kegan Paul, Trench, Trubner & Co, 1925), p. 82.

29. Watson, *Psychological Care of Infant and Child* (1928), quoted by Christina Hardyment, *Dream Babies: Child Care from Locke to Spock* (London: Jonathan Cape, 1983), p. 175.

30. Quoted by Hardyment, *Dream Babies*, p. 173.

31. Ekman, 'Afterword' to *The Expression of the Emotions*, p. 387.

32. Donald E. Brown, *Human Universals* (Philadelphia: Temple University Press, 1991).

33. Homer, *The Odyssey*, XXIII, trans. Robert Fagles (London and New York: Penguin, 1997), p. 458.

34. *The Odyssey*, trans. Fagles, p. 462.

35. *The Expression of the Emotions*, p. 360.

36. *Nature*, 409 (15 February 2001), p. 914.

II   Can science and literature collaborate
     to define human nature?

3   Literature and evolution

Joseph Carroll

The occasions and parts of this chapter

The audience at the 2004 symposium on 'Literature, Science and Human Nature' consisted both of academics and educated lay people. I was invited to participate in the symposium because I had published a book and a number of articles in which I had sought to integrate literary study with Darwinian social science.[1] In the talk I gave, I described the way I had arrived at Darwinian thinking, located my own intellectual history in the larger history of modern literary study, and sketched out the main features in my theory of literary meaning. In the second part of the chapter below, 'Coming home to human nature', I'll go back over the main points in that presentation.

To give a more interactive character to the symposium, the presenters were grouped into 'seminars' of twos or threes, and we were encouraged to engage in dialogue with one another and with the audience. I was paired off with the geneticist Gabriel Dover, and our seminar was entitled 'Can Science and Literature Collaborate to Define Human Nature?' Gabriel and I have distinctly different views on evolution, human nature and literature, so this pairing offered an occasion for some vigorous debate. Most of that debate took place in email exchanges before the symposium. To exploit the rhetorical advantages of a debate – the direct conversational speech and the stimulus of differing views – in the third part of this chapter, 'Human universals and individual identities in literature', I'll transcribe portions of the exchange with Gabriel. These comments should give a more vivid and particular sense of how I think human experience is absorbed into literary representation.

It is relatively easy to affirm that we can incorporate information from Darwinian psychology into our understanding of human nature and literary representation. It is more difficult to find ways to incorporate the actual methods of science into literary study: data collection, empirical testing, falsification. More difficult, but not impossible. In the fourth section of the chapter, 'Taking up the challenge of scientific method in literary study', I'll explore that question, suggest some possible solutions, and describe a collaborative project designed to help bring those solutions into reach.

Coming home to human nature

'What kind of knowledge am I ultimately supposed to produce?' When I was a student, some 30 years ago, that question did not at first present itself to me in a provocative way. My energies were sufficiently challenged by learning the skills of literary research, developing expertise in interpretive analysis, learning languages, and absorbing information about the philosophical and historical contexts of literature. None of this was science, exactly, but I took it for granted that science and literary study shared an ordinary respect for logic and fact. As I matured towards professional scholarly study, I became steadily more sensitive to the difficulties of contributing something new to knowledge and understanding. My earliest solutions to that challenge were twofold: on the one side to seek expansive scholarly contexts in intellectual history and 'comparative literature', and on the other side to delve into authors or texts that seemed particularly difficult or problematic, aiming to tease out structures of meaning that for one reason or another had not yet been adequately understood. (The spirit behind this latter strategy finds evocative literary expression in Henry James's story 'The Figure in the Carpet.') In my first book, on Matthew Arnold's cultural theory, I emphasized the first of these two strategies. In my second book, on the modern American poet Wallace Stevens, and in subsequent work on Walter Pater, I emphasized the second.

While I was following the trajectory I have described, the larger community of academic literary scholars was moving in a different direction.

During the middle decades of the twentieth century, academic literary study had been mainly divided into two fields of action: (a) basic scholarship for establishing texts, collecting letters and writing biographies; and (b) interpretive exegesis or the close reading of specific texts. In Victorian literature, my own field, signal instances of such basic scholarship include Gordon Haight on George Eliot, Leon Edel on Henry James, and R. H. Super on the prose works of Matthew Arnold. The close reading of specific texts – studies in imagery, tone and verbal structure – is associated particularly with the work of 'New Critics' such as Brooks and Warren in America and I. A. Richards and William Empson in England. The formalistic analyses of the New Critics had been extended and supplemented by ethical or moral content criticism such as that of F. R. Leavis and the Chicago Aristotelians.[2]

By the late 1970s, both forms of traditional criticism had begun to show signs of fatigue. The basic scholarship on most canonical authors had been completed. And the proliferation of formalistic 'readings' of individual texts had reached a point of rapidly diminishing returns. Saturation and repetition were leading to increasingly desperate and ingenious exercises in over-reading – fabricating imaginary figures in real carpets. The signal for a change of institutional strategy was clearly and effectively sounded in 1975 in Jonathan Culler's *Structuralist Poetics*.[3] Culler boldly identified the problem of saturation and pointed the way towards a vast new field of endeavour. Literary scholars should not, he recommended, continue to read literary texts. They should instead concentrate their commentary on the medium and method of linguistic signification. More specifically, they should devote their energies to assimilating and elaborating the theories of the Continental structuralists. This appeal had scarcely been made before structuralism was already obsolete; but the position assigned by Culler to the structuralists was also already occupied by the poststructuralists – by theorists such as Althusser, Derrida, Foucault, Lacan, Kristeva, Jameson and Fish – and the academic literary community migrated en masse into this new territory.

Literary exegesis did not cease, but it did take on a different look. Most traditional literary study, both scholarship and criticism, had presupposed that texts had determinate meanings and that the business of literary study was to explain or at least describe those meanings. In Matthew Arnold's redundantly emphatic phrase, the business of criticism was 'to see the object as in itself it really is'.[4] The new poststructuralist doctrines explicitly denied the reality of determinate meanings and instead absorbed literary texts within a universal field of perpetually shifting and self-cancelling semiotic activity. The object-in-itself-as-it-really-is ceased to exist, and the business of criticism became instead the effort to process any given text through some particular theoretical or critical idiom. Lacan's poststructuralist Freudianism gave psychological content to this enterprise; Althusser's poststructuralist Marxism gave it social content; and various forms of radical political affiliation – feminism, postcolonialism, multiculturalism, and queer theory – infused it with moral purpose and social passion.

The deepest ideological animus that united the intellectual and political impulses in poststructuralism was provided by Michel Foucault, and that animus provided also a common ideological stance or persona for the profession. Following Foucault, and citing him with a frequency and submissiveness like that with which the orthodox schoolmen cited Saint Thomas Aquinas, poststructuralist theorists envisioned all texts as media not of knowledge but of 'power'. In the discursive field defined by the Foucauldian poststructuralists, claims for determinate meanings associate themselves with the normative ideological values of dominant social groups – males, heterosexuals, colonial powers and the bourgeois elite – and poststructuralist 'demystification' associates itself with the subversive self-affirmations of social groups previously subordinated or suppressed.

Poststructuralist epistemology and ideology are universalizing. Under the poststructuralist banner, literary culture or humanistic scholarship no longer occupies its own special and distinct enclave within the faculty of the liberal arts. 'There is no outside the text.' Step outside the boundaries of deconstructive rhetorical analysis, and one simply falls off the face of the earth. Chemistry, physics, physiology? They are discourse, and yet more discourse – part of the whole mystified apparatus of phallologocentric domination imposed on an

the correspondence I receive, I know that many students and younger literary scholars are eager to take advantage of this information, but they are still finding it difficult to gain acceptance for their interests within the academic literary establishment. Within the next few years, there is a good chance that we shall have an opportunity to observe a new epistemic revolution. Meanwhile, those of us who have tenure and have managed to survive on the margins of the literary establishment will continue developing our own research programmes.

I'll briefly outline here the chief claims I have made about literature and human nature. I begin with 'evolutionary epistemology', the idea that the mind has evolved in an adaptive relation to the actual world and that it can give us reasonably adequate access to the world outside ourselves. I also emphasize the structural importance of the biological concepts of organism and environment and correlate those terms with the literary terms 'character' and 'setting'. The third chief element of literary representations is 'plot' or a connected sequence of events in which characters either achieve or fail to achieve fulfilment in their purposes. To delineate the content of those purposes, I make appeal to the idea of a limited and structured set of basic human behavioural dispositions: for survival, mating and reproduction, forming kin networks, negotiating complex social systems, manipulating technology, and constructing systems of meaning through forms such as narratives, art, music, myths, religions, ideologies, philosophies and science. I identify three levels for the organization of human motives: (a) elemental, species-typical dispositions; (b) the variable organization of those dispositions within specific cultural ecologies; and (c) the peculiarities of individual identity, as that identity is modulated through varying innate potentials and the accidents of individual experience. I emphasize that meaning in literature, as in life, is always located in some specific mind, and I draw a direct link between the individual mind and the literary concept of 'point of view'. I argue that literature or its oral antecedents are fundamentally social and communicative in nature, and I specify that literary meaning works itself out in the interactive relations among three points of view: that of the author, that of the characters depicted, and that of the audience. I note that literature takes as its central subject the nature of human experience and that it is suffused with subjective, affective sensation. I correlate affective sensation with 'tone' in literature, and in order to provide a scientific point of entry for the concept of 'tone' I invoke the theory of 'basic emotions' as delineated by Paul Ekman, Robert Plutchik and others.[7] To gain a scientific point of entry for the idea of individual identity, I invoke the most advanced current theory of personality: the theory of the Big Five personality factors, or the Five-Factor Model.[8] In discussing with evolutionary psychologists and other literary theorists the question as to whether the proclivity for producing and consuming literature is an evolved and adaptive behaviour, I reject the idea that literary behaviour is merely a by-product of other cognitive processes; I accept the idea, formulated by Steven Pinker and others, that literature can provide adaptively useful information, but I argue that the deeper adaptive function of literature is to provide an emotionally saturated image of the world in which we live. We use these images to organize and guide our complex motivational systems.[9] I maintain that the need to produce and consume aesthetic imaginative artefacts is as real and vital a need as the need to eat, to have sex, to tend offspring, and to develop and sustain relations within a social network.

Human universals and individual identities in literature

In our email exchange, Gabriel Dover's formulations prompted me to explain my views about how human experience enters into literary representations. I shall quote only as much of Gabriel's comments as are requisite to establish the occasion for my own remarks. Gabriel's views on such matters are given more scope in his own essay in this volume.

Traditionally, literary people have emphasized the qualitative and mysterious aspect of human experience, and people in science have inclined towards including human experience within the range of quantifiable phenomena that can be empirically tested. As Gabriel notes in one of the passages I'll quote below, one curious feature in our exchange is the reversal of these traditional roles.

I'll present the comments in dialogue form.

Gabriel Dover:

My main message will be that with reference to the all-important issue of the biological basis of individuality and the definition of human nature, the collaboration between biology and literature (the set theme of our joint session) is decidedly one-sided in that literature captures the essential unknowability of each individual phenotype in a way that biology has not with its generalized talk of 'universals'.

Joseph Carroll:

It looks as if we are well sorted for presenting issues for a discussion. We are concerned with some similar issues and come at them from somewhat different angles. For the past several years, I've been chiefly occupied with developing an adaptationist or Darwinian approach to literature. I've drawn heavily from sociobiology and evolutionary psychology but have also repeatedly criticized evolutionary psychologists and some Darwinian literary critics for discounting individuality and focusing too exclusively on 'human universals'. I don't think it would be possible in practice to predict the precise behaviour of any given individual, but I do believe that all behaviour and all mental experience are ultimately determined by a distinct causal network – a network that can be described as a set of interactions among organismic potentials ('innate' properties or dispositions) and environmental conditions. I agree that the precise configuration of these interactions at any given point in time is unique. That precise configuration has never existed before, if for no other reason than that one new element is always the cumulative force of all previous events, and that changes from moment to moment. Still, the scope that I would accord to individuality is probably considerably less, I would gather, than you would accord to it.

My own temperamental disposition is to believe quite strongly in individuality. When I was a child, I sometimes bemused myself with meditating on the hypothetical sensation of genuinely experiencing the qualitative subjectivity of some other person – any other person. At that time, I gave an emphasis to this qualitative difference much, much stronger than I would give it now. My supposition then was that if for even a single moment we could be placed inside the experiential field of another human being, the sense of alien strangeness would be so strong we might actually expire from sheer experiential shock. I now tend to think that in many of our characteristic modes of feeling and perceiving we are fairly similar to one another. I imagine in basic ways our sensations, passions and perceptions are largely interchangeable.

One of my chief concerns as a literary theorist and practical critic is to find good ways to talk simultaneously about the integration of identity on three levels: the level of shared elemental motives and dispositions ('human universals' or 'human nature'); the level of specific cultural configurations (Homeric Greece versus Victorian England versus medieval Japan, say); and the level of individual identity.

On the level of individual identity, I give a good deal of weight to peculiar genius, but even genius can be classed, I think, within specific parameters. The range of human variation is large but containable within definite categories.

Gabriel Dover:

There is the nub of an important difference between us regarding universals/individuality of human nature ... In fact it's rather amusing that as a card-carrying evolutionary geneticist I'm empirically opposed to any meaningful definition of human form/nature outside that central unit of biological organization we call the individual; whereas you, as a literary critic, wrap up individuality within the constraints of some ultimate (adaptively inspired) causal network based on shared features ...

In essence, I would argue against the three levels of identity that you describe (universals; culture; individual); and against your argument that differences in personalities are adaptive in meeting the needs of their 'evolved motive dispositions'.

Joseph Carroll:
Here are two key points on which we would disagree, with respect to individuality and human nature:

(a) I would argue that human nature or human universals or generalized concepts or pictures of human motives are always an active concern in literary representations. Literary depictions can be ranged on a scale, with highly abstract or generalized depictions at one end of the scale, and with highly individualized depictions at the other end. Some literary works – myths and allegories, for instance – clearly lodge towards the abstractive end. When a character in a medieval allegorical drama steps on to the stage and announces, 'I am Sin', we are not talking about a highly individualized personal identity. When Bunyan depicts his characters in *Pilgrim's Progress* as Christian, and Mr Worldly Wise Man, again, the emphasis is on the general. In modern realist fiction or modernist stream-of-consciousness narrative, there is a clear effort to evoke the particularity of an individual identity, modulated both by innate temperamental dispositions and also by the accidents of individual experience. Between these two extremes, most fiction takes place. The middle ground can be clearly observed in that kind of mixed fiction in which some characters are purely type characters and some characters are highly individualized. Fielding in *Joseph Andrews* or *Tom Jones* presents many characters whose very names identify their types as types, and he presents other characters who are very believably distinct individuals. Mr Allworthy is All Worthy, but Tom Jones and Mr Blifil are distinct individual persons. Dickens, Thackeray and Trollope do the same thing – with the mixing and blending of types and individuals. Sometimes a type emerges for a moment as an individual, with a vividly distinct centre of personal consciousness, and very often the highly individualized characters sink back into stereotypical patterns and formulaic responses. In *Middlemarch* Eliot presents the desiccated old scholar Casaubon from a number of perspectives. In the view of most characters, he is only a stereotype of the dull, plodding pedant. Eliot makes an explicit point of moving outside that perspective, moving inside Casaubon's own perspective, and evoking the individuality of his own sense of the world.

No character is either wholly generalized or wholly individualized. All allegorical characters are still individual characters – persons, first-person persons. It is Sin who says, 'I am Sin', but it is 'I' who makes that self-presentation. All individual characters share the common humanity of their form – not just their two legs and two eyes, but their common forms of orientation in space and time, perceptual faculties, modes of organizing concepts, and distinctly human ranges of feeling and value. No matter how highly individualized, every character is still also emblematic of elemental forms of feeling, thought and perception. Madame Bovary is an individual, but she is also a type. Prince André in *War and Peace* is an individual, but his social role is stereotypical; he never escapes from it, and his motives and responses are all easily calculable within the standard human repertory of ambition, love, jealousy and disgust.

(b) The sense of the universal or the elemental is an integral part of individual human experience. These are not isolable and separate components, such that one could say, 'Oh, literature is really only interested in individuals.' This too can be conceived as a polar continuum. People sense their peculiar individuality. I actually remember the first time I ever did. I was two years old, sitting in the back seat of a car. The car had been packed with goods and was towing a trailer, because the whole family was moving. The car was parked in a yard, for easier packing, and when it moved off, it went over the kerb stone and there was a sharp bounce. Being quite small, I bounced off the seat. At the top of the bounce, I became self-consciously aware for the first time in my life, glanced around for a microsecond, observed something to the effect, 'Oh, I'm alive', and settled back down. The emphasis in that statement was spread evenly across the personal pronoun and the predicate adjective. 'Oh, I'M alive', and 'Oh, I'm ALIVE'. There is a me, and that me is alive. Being alive is most peculiar. The point of this anecdote is that yes, the sense of individual identity is something distinct and important. Without it, there would be no literature, no art, nothing but the instinct-guided perceptual apparatus that presumably limits animal consciousness to its immediate sensory surround and the promptings of local action.

People sense their peculiar individuality. All thought and all feeling are contained within individual minds. If one gets carried away by this observation, as Walter Pater did, one might be tempted to make the false claim that every one of us is surrounded by a thick wall of personality through which no other living voice has ever penetrated. But Pater was a neurotic introvert suffering from the self-suppressed sexuality and isolation imposed on him by his position as an Oxford don. He didn't want to end up in jail like Oscar Wilde, and in any case, unlike Wilde, he simply had no talent either for gregariousness or for intimacy.

Pater was wrong. People do sense the experience of other people. It varies a lot from person to person. Differences in empathy are measurable. What one senses in other people is not just the ineffable peculiarity of their unique individuality. What one senses is the common medium of common perception, common thought, common passion. If people were truly 'unique' in any very radical way, it would not be possible for ordinary empathy, ordinary insight into others' minds, to take place. Moreover, even the sense of individual uniqueness is itself one of those human universals that we all recognize in one another. Paradoxically if you will, we all see that every one of us feels distinct. Each of us is a distinct centre of consciousness, feeling, desire and value. That recognition can be the basis for all civil behaviour and tolerance. It can also be used, in a Machiavellian way, to manipulate the gullible, to play on their vanity and credulity. No one has ever occupied my particular point in space and time before, or had the exact combination of neurochemical dispositions and the exact same sequence of personal experiences I have had, or that you have had, or that anyone has had. But your hunger is not much different from mine, your desire for friends or love, your sensitivity to charges against your own self-esteem – all that is as common as dirt, in you, me and everybody.

Art evokes particularity in sensation and identity. Yes. Art evokes elemental and common experience. Yes. One of the features of particular experience is that actual, subjective sensation of elemental experience. We don't just sense ourselves as peculiar and unique moments of feeling and observation. We recognize in our sensations the common animal urges, the elemental passions. That is in itself a feature of great art. I don't think much of pure allegory. Medieval religious dramas are comically simple-minded. And the ultra-individualized internal monologues of Virginia Woolf strike me as tiresome and effete. My own standards of artistic response, and the active standards of many people in our modern Western culture, require both universality and individuality in highly developed forms. We need the sense of highly individualized identity because that is one of the hypertrophic features of our own culture (markedly different from that of many tribal societies, and different even from that of some traditional but highly developed Asian societies), but we also yearn for the sense of archetypal depth. Wallace Stevens and Yeats actively and consciously created new modern mythologies, new archetypal pantheons, connecting us once again with the elemental properties of earth – of time, and night and day, and the seasons, and the weather – and also with the elemental properties of human nature, with the yearning of infants for maternal warmth, the passion of tenderness for women, the exaltation of heroism, and the brooding terror of death. They created mythic figures who emblematized such elemental forces, and invested them with personal identity.

Taking up the challenge of scientific method in literary study

Literary Darwinism offers some new challenges and opportunities to interpretive literary exegesis. It offers new insight into the power and validity of some traditional concepts of literary analysis – character, setting, plot, point of view, and symbolism – and it also suggests new contexts of empirical analysis in which those concepts can be explored and developed. 'Character' is the largest content category, and it invites research into the fields of adaptationist psychology: for instance, into developmental psychology, sex differences, mating strategies, family dynamics, social life, emotions and personality. Plot is formed out of actions based on human motives, and study of character extends into the understanding of plot. Plot and character both feed into symbolism, and the study of symbolic meaning should gain a new impetus from the cognitive neurosciences. Point of view is the chief locus of literary meaning – meaning is always meaning for someone – and the scientific study of point of view now has a broad thoroughfare opened to it in the theory of 'theory of mind' and 'empathy' to which Simon Baron-Cohen has made major contributions.

Providing new materials for literary exegesis is a legitimate goal of Darwinian literary study, but if that study were to stop there it would not have proceeded, methodologically, past the point at which old-fashioned Marxist and Freudian criticism used to operate – the point at which a putatively scientific vocabulary is used for intuitive and speculative commentary that remains outside the range of ideas that can be tested and falsified. If all Darwinian criticism did was to offer a new vocabulary of interpretive concepts, it would have made some advance; it would have advanced to just that extent to which Darwinian social science is an advance over Freudian psychology and Marxist sociology. But it would still be mired in that range of 'knowledge' in which validity is submerged within cogency, and cogency depends exclusively on the force of assertion, the credulity of response, or the consensus of an orthodoxy.

How do we break through this barrier? We must find ways to bring literary concepts and interpretive hypotheses within the range of testable propositions. One such possibility presents itself in cognitive neuroscience. 'Theory of Mind' is no longer merely theoretical. Research in neuroendocrinology and neuroimaging brings this concept into the range of study susceptible to empirical testing, and there is no good reason that we should not soon find ingenious ways of including literary responses in the phenomena that are thus tested.[10] Another possibility presents itself in the statistical analysis of literary content ('content analysis') and literary response. In the space remaining to me here, I'll give a brief description, by way of example, of one such project.

Jon Gottschall, a young literary scholar, developed a method for analysing human universals in large numbers of folk and fairy tales from diverse cultures. He also conducted a 'census' of signal features of characters in Western canonical literature.[11] Gottschall and I recently adapted this method to the analysis of the characteristics of protagonists and antagonists in Victorian novels – analysing motives, mate preferences and personal qualities.[12] The results from this initial study were intriguing enough to encourage us to undertake a larger, more ambitious project along similar lines. In company with Maryanne Fisher and Ian Jobling, the psychologist Dan Kruger had already developed a method for assessing the response of readers to characters who exemplify different sexual strategies in literary works.[13] Kruger and another psychologist, John Johnson, are now collaborating with us in setting up a questionnaire on the web. (Johnson is a personality psychologist with extensive experience in web-based questionnaire research).[14] We shall be soliciting ratings of motives, mate preferences and personality for characters in Victorian novels. The website lists about 2,100 characters from about 200 novels (Austen to Forster).

Using the responses we get from these questionnaires, we anticipate being able to draw significant conclusions about the depictions of male and female sexual identity, about motives and mate preferences, and about the characteristics of protagonists and antagonists in the novels. From those conclusions we can make strong inferences about the normative value structures among writers and readers in the period. We shall also be comparing depictions by male and female authors and responses in male and female readers. The data we collect and the conclusions we draw from them will be contributions to a relatively new branch of social science – the empirical study of literary representation. The knowledge thus obtained should have an intrinsic value and interest, and it should also provide a framework of empirical knowledge about the novels of the period. That framework should provide guidance and constraint for the examination of structures of meaning within individual novels, authors, or groups of novels and authors.

Notes

1. Joseph Carroll, *Evolution and Literary Theory* (Columbia, MO: University of Missouri Press, 1995). All but the most recent articles have now been collected in Joseph Carroll, *Literary Darwinism: Evolution, Human Nature, and Literature* (New York: Routledge, 2004).

2. See M. H. Abrams, 'The Transformation of English Studies: 1930–1995', *Daedalus*, 126 (1997), pp. 105–32.

3. Jonathan Culler, *Structuralist Poetics: Structuralism, Linguistics, and the Study of Literature* (Ithaca: Cornell University Press, 1975).

4. Matthew Arnold, 'On Translating Homer', in *The Classical Tradition*, ed. R. H. Super, *The Complete Prose Works of Matthew Arnold*, 11 vols (Ann Arbor: University of Michigan Press, 1960–77), Vol. 1 (1960), p. 140.

5. Paul R. Gross and Norman Levitt, *Higher Superstition: The Academic Left and Its Quarrels with Science* (Baltimore, MD: Johns Hopkins University Press, 1994); Alan D. Sokal, 'Transgressing the Boundaries: Toward a Transformative Hermeneutics of Quantum Gravity', *Social Text*, 14 (1996), pp. 217–52.

6. For surveys of this literature, see Harold Fromm, 'The New Darwinism in the Humanities: From Plato to Pinker', *Hudson Review*, 56 (2003), pp. 89–99; Harold Fromm, 'The New Darwinism in the Humanities: Back to Nature, Again', *Hudson Review*, 56 (2003), pp. 315–27; Joseph Carroll, *Literary Darwinism*, pp. 11–22; Joseph Carroll, 'Evolutionary Psychology and Literary Study', in David Buss (ed.), *Handbook of Evolutionary Psychology* (New York: Wiley, forthcoming). Also see Jonathan Gottschall and David Sloan Wilson (eds), *The Literary Animal: Evolution and the Nature of Narrative* (Evanston, IL: Northwestern University Press, forthcoming).

7. Paul Ekman, *Emotions Revealed: Recognizing Faces and Feelings to Improve Communication and Emotional Life* (New York: Henry Holt, 2003); Robert Plutchik, *Emotions and Life Perspectives from Psychology,*

Biology, and Evolution (Washington, DC: American Psychological Association, 2003).

8. See David Buss, 'Social Adaptation and Five Major Factors of Personality', in Jerry S. Wiggins (ed.), *The Five-Factor Model of Personality: Theoretical Perspectives* (New York: Guilford Press, 1996), pp. 180–207; Gerard Saucier and Louis Goldberg, 'The Language of Personality: Lexical Perspectives on the Five-Factor Model', in Jerry S. Wiggins (ed.), *The Five-Factor Model of Personality: Theoretical Perspectives* (New York: Guilford Press, 1996), pp. 21–50; Jerry Wiggins and Paul Trapnell, 'Personality Structure: The Return of the Big Five', in Robert Hogan, John Johnson and Stephen Briggs (eds), *Handbook of Personality Psychology* (San Diego: Academic Press, 1997), pp. 737–65; Oliver P. John and Sanjay Srivastava, 'The Big Five Trait Taxonomy: History, Measurement, and Theoretical Perspectives', in Lawrence Pervin and Oliver P. John (eds), *Handbook of Personality*, 2nd edn (New York: Guilford Press, 1999), pp. 102–38.

9. In addition to the essays in *Literary Darwinism*, see Joseph Carroll, 'The Adaptive Function of Literature', in Colin Martindale, Paul Locher and Leonid Dorfman (eds), *Evolutionary and Neurocognitive Approaches to the Arts* (Amityville, NY: Baywood Publishing, forthcoming).

10. For a commentary that assimilates recent neuroscience advances in theory of mind with a comprehensive model for the evolution of human intelligence, see Mark V. Flinn, David C. Geary and Carol V. Ward, 'Ecological Dominance, Social Competition, and Coalitionary Arms Races: Why Humans Evolved Extraordinary Intelligence', *Evolution and Human Behavior* (forthcoming).

11. Jonathan Gottschall, *et al.*, 'Patterns of Characterization in Folk Tales Across Geographic Regions and Levels of Cultural Complexity: Literature as a Neglected Source of Quantitative Data', in *Human Nature*, 14 (2003), pp. 365–82; Jonathan Gottschall, *et al.*, 'Results of an Empirical Search for the Virgin-Whore Dichotomy', in *Interdisciplinary Literary Study*, 6 (2004), in press; Jonathan Gottschall, *et al.*, 'Sex Differences in Mate Choice Criteria are Reflected in Folktales from around the World and in historical European Literature', in *Evolution and Human Behavior*, 25 (2004), pp. 102–12; Jonathan Gottschall, *et al.*, 'A Census of the Western Canon: Literary Studies and Quantification', under submission.

12. Joseph Carroll and Jonathan Gottschall, 'Human Nature and Agonistic Structure in Canonical British Novels of the Nineteenth and Early Twentieth Centuries: A Content Analysis', in Uta Klein, Katja Mellmann and Steffanie Metzger (eds), *Anthropologie und Sozialgeschichte der Literatur Heuristiken der Literaturwissenschaft* (Paderborn, Germany: Mentis Verlag, forthcoming). For a summary of other studies in the quantitative, empirical analysis of literature, see Robin Dunbar, 'Why Are Good Writers so Rare? An Evolutionary Perspective on Literature', *Journal of Evolutionary and Cultural Psychology* (forthcoming).

13. Daniel Kruger, Maryanne Fisher and Ian Jobling, 'Proper and Dark Heroes as Dads and Cads: Alternative Mating Strategies in British and Romantic Literature', *Human Nature*, 14 (2003), pp. 305–17.

14. See   http://www.personal.psu.edu/faculty/j/5/j5j/IPIP/   (accessed 27/11/04).

4   Human nature: one for all and all for one?[1]

Gabriel Dover

Some words on DNA and Darwin's nose

The extent to which DNA has penetrated our collective culture is illustrated with the hanging of the portrait of Sir John Sulston, a leading explorer of the human genome, in the National Portrait Gallery, London. But there is no figurative image of Sir John to be seen; instead we are treated to a display of numerous bacterial growths on an appropriate nutrient, each of which contains a cloned section of Sir John's DNA. The Gallery states that:

> the portrait offers an exact representation of the sitter, because it contains the minute differences along the length of his genome that make Sir John unique. It is the most realist portrait in the Gallery since it carries the actual instructions – the 'recipe' – that led to the creation of John. It is a portrait of his parents, and every ancestor he ever had back to the beginning of Life in the universe.

In what follows I argue that the idea of an exact, repeatable link between Sir John's DNA (genotype) and his form and behaviour (phenotype) is wholly misconceived. There is no genetic blueprint in Sir John's genotype with an instruction 'go forth, and make me Sir John', as we know and admire him. The unique phenotype that is Sir John has indeed emerged from his unique genotype but that too, as I argue, is beside the point. Something had to emerge (all things being dandy with the future progress of a particular fertilized egg) as an inevitable outcome of a complex and unpredictable process of development – but did that something have to be the unique phenotype of Sir John that did happen to emerge?

The widespread assumption that we can trace a direct and inevitable line between genotype and phenotype is no different in kind from that of Captain Fitzroy, who nearly rejected Darwin joining him on the *Beagle* on account of the shape of his nose which, Fitzroy claimed, was indicative of a man who did not possess sufficient energy and determination for the voyage. Whether from DNA or from noses, dubious predictions are two a penny.

The development of John's mother's fertilized egg, containing two human genomes, one with an X and one with a Y chromosome, produces willy-nilly a human male that is not only a member of the human species, but is also a particular, uniquely formed male emerging as one of many potential, uniquely formed males. Sir John arose out of a process of 'individualization' (personalization) that is not inscribed in his genotype, and which could have been otherwise.

Universality and particularity sit side by side in the phenomenon that is biology – and all without the help of a set of DNA instructions for the formulation of either a general member of a species or any particular path of personalization that goes into the making of any particular member.

So how is this done? And how does the reality of biology, as it cycles ceaselessly from one generation of phenotypes to the next, impinge on our debate on the origins and evolved causes of human nature?

Some words on undirected development

A population of biological organisms is unlike a population of water molecules: there are no regularities of events from which universal and timeless laws can be drawn. This chalk and cheese difference is overlooked by those engaged in the mathematical analysis of evolving populations in which partial genotypes (sometimes as little as a single gene) are the fixed units of consideration, rather than, as Darwin taught us, whole phenotypes and their messy habits. In every sexual species new phenotypes arise in every generation that have never before existed and that will never exist again.

How and why do phenotypes differ, and why do such differences not transcend the species barrier? In other words, why do fertilized human eggs consistently produce human and not, say, chimp phenotypes when there are no inscribed instructions for the making of either humans or chimps?

Many biologists would answer this question with metaphors of the 'control' or 'regulation' of genes as they are switched on or off at different stages and in different cells. The assumption here is that such patterns of switching are directed by species-specific control circuits leading to the emergence of species-specific form and behaviour during the development of each individual. The shaping of individuals into human (or chimp) phenotypes is indeed a consequence of turning genes on or off in patterns that are species-specific; however, there is nothing in the human (or chimp) genome that controls or regulates what needs to happen sequentially and positionally, either in the sense of an identifiable blueprint or with respect to the more relaxed image of a recipe. Is there a problem here?

Undirected, and yet determined, development occurs throughout the living world. The paradox is solved when we consider all species as having evolved from one original source some three and a half billion years ago. Darwin's image of a single tree of life connecting all extinct and extant species by links that reflect evolved patterns of ancestry and descent is instructive. This metaphor of a tree of evolved relationships underlines the important point that we should not be surprised at the absence of species-specific 'regulatory' networks at the outermost tips of the grand tree of life. Rather we should be thinking of on–off patterns of gene switching as being lineage-specific.

For example, the complex biochemical process that ensures that a string of amino acids in a given protein precisely corresponds with the string of nucleotide bases in a given gene (a process known as 'translation of the genetic code') is shared by all living organisms (animals, plants, fungi, bacteria and viruses), and became established through trial and error at the base of the tree. Hence, the operation of the genetic code in humans is a result of a particular pattern of on–off gene switching that can be traced backwards through the lineage of bifurcations that took place since the origin of life.

The same is true of many widely shared processes by which, say, cells pass chemical messages from one to another, or that control when and where cells divide. Other biological phenomena that are restricted to particular lineages of the tree arose later in evolution; for example, the processes by which sexual division and fusion occurs at the cellular level, or the rise of multicellular organisms with specialized cells. Some processes are so recent that they are restricted to single species on the smallest twigs: for example language and sentience in humans.

Let us suppose, then, that during the establishment of the process of 'translation' it became essential for gene A (and its corresponding protein) chemically to interact with gene B (and its corresponding protein). Let us also suppose that as a consequence of the A/B interaction, elements C and F interact, and that in turn leads to the interaction of elements M, J and T and so forth. After a series of sequential interactions has taken place in the right order and in the right places, involving tens upon tens of elements, the appropriate cellular machinery is in place to interpret the genetic code. It might well have been different in that an alternative set of interactions might have gotten established in those early stages of life as a consequence of chance and necessity. But I will not follow this digression. The point here is that the extant, universal genetic code (and its very minor deviations) is what Francis Crick has called a 'frozen accident'; and there is no requirement for an inscribed 'regulatory programme' specifying the order and placing of interactions required for this process.

Gene A interacts first with B because that is what successfully happened at the origin, and all subsequent genomes of all species kick off with the A/B interaction if they want to establish a cellular machinery to translate the established genetic code. A is not 'instructed' to interact with B. There is an inevitable occurrence of the requisite A/B interaction, and all other subsequent interactions, during the short time span of development that reflects events established on an evolutionary timescale. When evolution and development are so intimately enmeshed one with another, in that strange yet successful phenomenon we call biology, who needs regulatory programmes, blueprints and recipes? The transformation of a human genotype into a human phenotype occurs willy-nilly given that the structure and sequence of the human genome retain a memory of events having taken root during billions of years of evolution from the origin to the present.

Some words on not being the same and the rise of the blank slate

There is a danger in the above argument that we might be led to assume that all human fertilized eggs, containing evolved human genomes, would produce the same human phenotype. Judgements as to sameness or difference depend, however, on the starting perspective. From the viewpoint of a chimp, all humans are the same, circumscribed by a 'universal' form and nature, isolated on a single twig of the tree of life. From the viewpoint of a single human, every individual is different in all aspects of form and behaviour that nevertheless characterize the species as a whole.

As Darwin recognized, evolution takes effect on the back of individual differences. Hence, if we desire to understand human form and nature from either a developmental or evolutionary vantage point then we had better take care of individual particularities. Biology does not really deal in 'elemental universals' or time-honoured 'genetic programmes of regulation', as such. Our ultimate goal is to unpick, no matter how seemingly hopeless a task, the intricate weave of evolution and development that goes into the construction of an individual phenotype. When biologists resort to generalization rather than particularization it is often due to a combination of experimental limitations and casual thinking, both of which are rectifiable as time moves on.

Biologists could do no better than turn to the producers and consumers of our more perceptive works of literature to appreciate the central importance of the individual, more of which I discuss later. For the moment I offer the summary that, *from the perspective of a chimp*, there is a commonly shared and definable human form and nature, but these cannot be realized outside of the millions upon millions of individual takes on such species-specific features; that is, outside of the singularities of each human, as he/she emerged from a unique path of development reflecting a lineage of events that go back to the Big Origin.

There are two major causes of our differences: sex and networks. Although I need to be brief, they deserve attention in that the first somewhat dispels the notion that we do not start off as a 'blank slate'; and the second teaches us that the process of development and the emergence of each individual's human nature is essentially unpredictable and unknowable.

Sex has the peculiar habit of breaking up successful combinations of genes whose interactions led to a viable and fertile individual phenotype. There are many theoretical attempts doing the rounds to understand what might be the evolutionary advantages of such sexual demolition – none of which is fully satisfactory. What is clear, however, is that there are two rounds of genetic shuffling occurring during sex that ensure that the next generation of fertilized eggs contains combinations of genes that are unlike their contributing parents. The first involves the mechanics by which chromosomes (and hence genes) are randomly distributed to individual sperm and eggs such that no two sperm and no two eggs are genetically alike; and the second involves the fact that any sperm can fertilize any egg.

It is out of such specific genetic permutations that a variety of cellular processes, involving multitudes of genetic interactions, have to be reassembled. In other words, genes (technically alleles) that have never before co-existed in quite the same way in each new individual have to interact successfully one with another in the making of a viable and fertile phenotype that can then engage in a further round of the sexual shoe shuffle. There is a sense here, at least at the genetic level, of a sexually produced blank slate on which the networks of interactions have to be endlessly renegotiated, generation after generation.

What then is all this renegotiation about? At the heart of it is the requirement to set up what are termed 'scale-free' networks.[2] These are non-random networks of linked, interactive elements (networks of genes; of proteins; of metabolites; and so on) that contain a higher than expected number of elements with very high numbers of interactive links, surrounded by elements with just a handful of links. The multilinked hubs are not unlike the main railway stations in the network of stations of the London Underground. Hence, the establishment of a major feature of human phenotype, such as cell–cell signalling, the heart, consciousness, language and so on, requires a specific topology of interactions and a specific quality of interaction at each link between two and more elements.

Significantly, many elements are highly promiscuous and participate in many different networks; they can usefully be envisaged as particular pieces of Lego® that can go into the making of many different structures. Indeed, there is evidence that small sub-networks involving a handful of fixed elements, highly connected within a defined topology, also participate in a large number of different, larger networks.

The existence of both multilinked hubs and of widely shared elements and sub-networks among the differing developmental operations provides both stability and flexibility during the sexual merry-go-round of construction and deconstruction.

Some words on the abstraction of the 'universal, average individual'

The particular course taken by a unique combination of genes in the setting up of a network is specific to an individual; and the particular course actually taken is only one of many that might have been taken, given the complexities and fluidity in what has to be done. A human (and not a chimp) phenotype emerges whatever the course taken; however, each and every individual is a different take on human form and behaviour. There is little to be gained (and much that is thrown away) with concepts of average or normal or natural or universal or elemental human form and behaviour: there are only millions upon millions of instances of unexpected ('unnatural') individual takes. We are all monsters now! Each is born with two legs, but it's each individual's particular take on the theme of two legs, as they emerged from a particular, personalized path of development, that is the relevant singularity of interest to our scientific and literary curiosity.

The same argument applies to any of the 400 and more constituents that comprise so-called 'universal human nature'. Literary reliance on species-specificity and commonality leads to a cul-de-sac of truisms bordering on tautologies. Such abstractions neither produce nor illuminate very much beyond their own generalities, (Hey! Look where we are on the evolved tree of life.). In all likelihood the rise of oral literature in the human species has to be (for there is no obvious alternative) a consequence of unique individual authors narrating the lives of unique characters to unique phenotypes of listeners. As all units in this chain of effects are members of the human species, each reflects a unique combination of features of what it means to be human on a specific twig of the tree of life.

We can depict each individual as a switchboard of hundreds of variable dimmer-switches, each representing an identifiable feature of human form and behaviour. The vagaries of sex and development ensure that each switch has been set at a different level in each individual, with the potential to alter settings throughout an individual lifespan.

With what else can literature play (setting aside the world of science fiction), if not the variable settings of individual switchboards, encompassing the individualities of the producers, characters and consumers of literature? If marital bliss and marital spats are to be listed as a common, universal aspect of the human condition (from Homer's *Odyssey* to Joyce's *Ulysses*), then we take this as read, as we seek to be individually entertained by specific marital games in the minds of our individual authors. The same need for detail and nuance would apply to any of the other grand life-history traits (growth; sex; reproduction; death) of individual humans as they patiently sit out their portion of life on the common twig of the species. For a difference in emphasis on the relevance of species-typical characteristics in the overall human endeavour of literature, read Joseph Carroll's chapter in this book.

Some words on an expanded notion of nurture

From all that I've written above, a reader could be forgiven for concluding that despite my caveats and cautionary tales on the role of
genes in development and evolution I am a closet genetic determinist
for not having spent more than a couple of words on the concept of
nurture, as it is widely and persistently set up in false opposition to the
concept of nature. A close reading of the above, however, would reveal
that everything that I have described concerning the phenomenology
of genetic interactions during development speaks up for the primacy
of nurture. I am prepared to argue that nurture is the sole actor in the
unfolding drama of human form and behaviour, as it is in all other life
forms.

There is only nurture. This might come as a surprise to readers
of the latest two substantial offerings on the nature–nurture debate
from Steven Pinker[3] and Matt Ridley,[4] but not to followers of Susan
Oyama, the philosopher of biology who has done much to rethink
our basic concepts when contemplating the true significance of sex,
as organisms deconstruct and then reconstruct themselves, from one
generation to the next.[5] In what follows I accept Oyama's proposal in
general, although I provide a different set of supporting details stemming from our modern understanding of genetic operations.

To an extent, the definition of nurture is enmeshed in the shifting
usages of nature, of which there are three. The first usage is as in
Mother Nature: the external world of environment and landscape. The
second usage, as in the nature–nurture controversy, refers to something internal and constant, in opposition to the shifting external
world of nurture. In this second usage nurture has taken over the role
of nature in the first usage, if a little wider in its application. The third
usage is as in human nature – a product of nature (the second usage)
and nurture (also the second usage, having replaced nature in its first
usage).

Despite the fun to be had with these slippery definitions, there is a
serious problem with the third usage in that nature appears on both
sides of the developmental equation: it is both a cause ('nature', second

usage – implying genotype) and effect (the 'nature' of the emerging phenotype). This really won't do if clarity and common ground is to be sought as to the causes of human nature and how best they are represented in science and literature. In what follows I use nature as phenotype – indeed millions of natures reflecting millions of individual processes of undirected, yet determined, personalized development at each new generation. Where I need to refer to nature as in the second usage, I refer to genes, genotypes and genomes.

An argument can be made that there is no such thing as nature in its second usage in that, as I have briefly described above, the effect of a gene can only emerge through its interactions with other genes: an individual gene has no meaningful function that can be the separate, autonomous target of selection (other than in the abstract mathematics of population geneticists and in the lyrical metaphors of Richard Dawkins).[6]

The significance of this fact of life is that from the perspective of a single gene, all of its subsequent interactions with the relevant other genes in the specific networks in which it participates are its nurturing environment. This instantaneous environment of other relevant genes is no different in kind from the many other internal and external influences on a given gene, from mother's milk to atmospheric oxygen. The milieu of around 30,000 human genes is an important component of the processes of nurturing involved in the specific realization of a given gene in the emergence of an individual phenotype.

As the combinations of 30,000 genetic variations differ from fertilized egg to fertilized egg, there are millions of separate processes of nurturization, each of which ultimately produces a unique individual human form and nature. Indeed, the number of potential individuals far exceeds the combinatorial possibilities of 30,000 genes because of the variety of paths that can be taken through the networks of interaction that I have described. Several other cellular phenomena such as 'differential gene splicing', 'translational modification', 'protein chaperones' and so on, also add their substantial pennyworth to the generation of phenotypic variation, which I have not described.

This concept of an expanded, all-consuming process of nurturing that I am proposing underlies the developmental process of personalization, embracing many interacting components of genes, cellular constituents and environmental factors. As such, we cannot presently determine (what may prove to be unfathomable) the relative contributions of these components in the making of an individual phenotype. Modern biology is rendering obsolete the old simplistic definitions of nature and nurture. We can make general statements, and modern experimental biology is proud of many of the statements that it can make regarding the development of humans and other species – but only the surface is being scratched. The real, long-term fulfilment is to understand why, developmentally and evolutionarily, we are each different with respect to legs and sentience and marital spats, and how such differences inform and influence us in fact and fiction.

Some words on the significance of individuality

Individual differences are not just the peripheral and uninteresting variation imposed by a fluctuating environment on a hard, genetically determined, central core of universal humanness. A growing recognition of the origins and significance of individual differences is emerging from several quarters, and undoubtedly there will be more.

The first signs of this changing perspective are coming from within the medical sciences. First, there is the growing body of evidence that diseases supposedly affected by a single variant genetic element are dependent for their clinical manifestation on the total genetic background of the phenotype under consideration. This is true of *all* genetically influenced diseases including cystic fibrosis, muscular dystrophy and the globin blood disorders. The list is endless. For example, carriers of the precise same mutation in a given globin gene reveal a range of severity of clinical disorder from none at all through to individuals requiring constant blood transfusion. They all carry the identical mutant gene and produce the corresponding identical mutant protein, but the future influences such a protein might exert on development depend on what the rest of the non-globin genes might be doing, as they too participate in the relevant nurturing networks of individual phenotypes.[7]

Furthermore, influential drug companies are beginning to admit that most products do not work on most individuals, and that the only way forward is to design drugs that are cognizant of the genetic background of the individual and of the particular nurturing networks set up during the making of that individual's phenotype. I would contend that the totality of knowledge required for such specificity of drug action may be unachievable, given the undirected constructions of scale-free networks of interactions.

Secondly, a welcome if surprising other source of recognition of the significance of unique individual development is to be found in the analyses of variance of phenotypes for many human traits such as height, IQ and dozens of others with bell-shaped distributions – an analysis usually aimed at measuring the extent to which the genetic component (heritability) contributes to the range of phenotypes under observation, and to the potential range of phenotypes at the next generation.

In humans all such studies rely on measurements of similarity between individuals that have developed and been raised in different regimes: for example, genetically identical twins raised in the same or separate families, or adopted versus biological children raised in the same family, and so on. The point I draw attention to is the one emphasized by Steven Pinker that up to half the variation displayed for any given trait cannot be accounted for by either a shared nurture or a shared nature.[8] Instead, each individual is what he or she is, as a consequence of a component of what Pinker terms the 'unique environment' of an individual. Pinker does not know what precisely lies behind this component, but his own sharp instincts tell him that it cannot be ignored by psychologists and sociologists trying to understand the roles of parents, peer groups and culture as a whole on individual phenotypes.

In other words, I understand Pinker to be saying that there is a process of individualization, influenced by an individual's unique environment, that stubbornly emerges, come what may. And there is not a lot that can be done about it. Any parent faced with distinctly different children will recognize the truth of this observation, even if it has generally been forgotten in the throes of the nature–nurture controversy.

Other scholars when faced with the same observations might argue that the underlying cause of individuality is not the unique environment but rather the unique genotype of the individual, given the randomization consequences of sex and the establishment of the interactive networks that I have described. Others might opt for an ongoing interaction between nature and nurture.[9] My contention is that none of these attempts at an explanation is appropriate in that all of them rely on the assumed existence of two separate components.

There is indeed a core of individuality – particular and singular – that is the essence of each individual – formed by a process of personalized nurturing from the first stirrings of development in each and every fertilized egg. However, *nurturing involves the genes* as much as the involvement of all other components in a cell's internal and external environment, in the ways I have outlined.

There is no room in the phenomenology of biology for oppositions to be erected: nature *v* nurture (old definitions); external *v* internal; ultimate *v* proximal causes; elemental *v* local; common *v* singular; objective *v* subjective. The process of comprehensive nurturing that underlies the process of individualization in each new generation is the central happening of evolved organisms experiencing sex. Individual human nature is an inevitable yet unpredictable phenotypic outcome of unique combinations of mutually nurturing components.[10]

All we have in biology are individuals. It is crucial for literature, if it is truly to reflect and comment artistically on our evolved natures, to recognize the totality of sources involved in the particular path of nurturing that goes into the making of each individual, from the seeming blank slate generated by sex through to the all-singing, all-dancing individual.

This is not a demand for the producers of literature actually to understand nurturization in any given individual – after all, they cannot be expected to understand what is largely a black-box for the biologists – but is a call, rather, to recognize that a given individual's take on any one of the accepted features of 'human nature' is more important in the mechanics of evolution than vague concepts of 'universal and elemental essences' of nature that embrace the species as a whole. I believe that literature has long recognized the force of the former over the latter and that it has always been engaged, mostly unknowingly, with what we now call literary Darwinism.

Some words on 'literary Darwinism'

All literature, in dealing with the real world of evolved humans and their place in the universe, is a commentary in a Darwinian vein. Such artistic and philosophical commentary began thousands of years before the advent of the more recently delineated Darwinian view. Our modern-day hominid form and behaviour, and the self-awareness that comes with modern *Homo sapiens*, stretches back in time some two million years. We did not need Darwin to tell us that humans are biological entities, no different in kind from all other living creatures with the urge to consume, metabolize, excrete and reproduce. Furthermore, it did not need the advent of genetics for early ancestral parents to discern that their progeny were more similar to themselves than they were to unrelated others, and that, in keeping with all other non-human parents, they had more interest in the survival of their immediate progeny than that of others.

We can safely assume that along with all of this check on reality was the overarching, conscious recognition by our ancestors that every individual was different. All are upright and have bilateral symmetry but the range seemed endless and the uses to which such variable forms could be put in the biological business of individual survival and reproduction had a corresponding endlessness. What can be said about form in the minds of our modern human ancestors can also be said about behaviour, or about what some prefer to generalize as 'universal human nature'. Ambition, jealousy, anger, curiosity, aggression, cooperation, altruism and love – to pick on a handful of the hundreds of traits that go into 'human nature' – were undoubtedly recognized as shared by every individual, but it could be seen that each was nevertheless different in the dimmer-switch settings of all such features.

The recognition of individuality, and the ability to read the mind of another person, would have had far-reaching consequences for the ways modern *Homo sapiens* individuals were 'forced' to negotiate with one another in the business of survival and reproduction. It probably did not take long for literary narrative to reflect such basic biological understanding in the minds of our early Darwinian ancestors. I maintain that literature was rarely overly concerned with the biological truisms of 'elemental universals', but busied itself rather with the fascinating and instructive permutations of endlessly variable interactions between singular human natures, as they arose from sex-induced blank slates. (I regard the use of religious and ceremonial allegories as a special case.) Literature seems always and inescapably to have been composed in an arena of what we now recognize as the Darwinian world of ever-changing individual entities, and not the artificial set pieces of archetypes and stereotypes. What alternative could there be if infinitely variable human phenotypes were composing the narratives?

Some words on cranky subjectivity

Finally, I spend the last of my allotted words on the enjoyable pastime of the pejorative of personal preference, as my phenotype enacts the inescapable process of unique and comprehensive nurturing that happened to shape my unique combination of inherited genes into specific networks of interactions. My phenotype interacts with the unique phenotypes that arose in the imaginations of unique authors: one outcome of which is that my preference for, and private interpretation of, a given narrative is, like everyone else's, a subjective phenomenon that cannot be passed on to another, with the words at our disposal. Cranky subjectivity is all that we might have by way of Darwinian literary criticism – but we are in good company, for the subjectivity of 'qualia' and a sense of oneself are the central unsolved problems of philosophers of mind.

I was once invited by the *Guardian* newspaper to choose a book that changed my life. I wrote the following:

Ten lifetimes and ten marriages ago, I descended into the deepest spot on earth to bulldoze dykes across the Dead Sea. This was badlands peopled by Steinbeck: ex-kibbutz peasants (like myself), Druze Arabs and lone adventurers. Down in the cauldron of heat we gave the lie to the belief that animals live in the 'eternal present', whilst humans suffer the sentience of their past, present and future existence. We were men without a past or future. We laboured in the 'eternal present' of the relentless sun, alone yet strangely bound together. Camus would have recognized that. But it was prissy Virginia Woolf's *The Waves*, with its seamless lyricism and insight into the essential solitude of the human condition which became my companion.

In the blackness of each night shift, astride the screeching bulldozer, stranded between sea and shore, I learned to smell the first, faint signs of the new dawn long before the sun rose over the Jordanian hills. '*Gradually as the sky whitened a dark line lay on the horizon dividing the sea from the sky and the grey cloth became barred with thick strokes moving one after another, beneath the surface, following each other, pursuing each other, perpetually.*'

The book's overarching structure has the shape of the birth and death of a single day, each phase interspersed with a mosaic of monologues of a group of friends, describing their lives from child to adult, and each sensing the illogicality yet beauty of separate existences. ' "*Now they have all gone*", said Louis. "*I am alone. I hold a stalk in my hand. I am the stalk. My roots go down to the depths of the world through veins of red and silver, I am all fibre . . . up here my eyes are green leaves, unseeing*".'

Woolf's characters are as trapped in the 'eternal present' of each moment of their lives, at each phase of the sun, as were we poor buggers down in creation's muckpile. I don't know if the book changed my life, but my life changed the book.[11]

I suppose that what I wrote at that time and place is as subjective an exposure of my *self* as I can get, short of attaching a naked photograph. And yet this does not reveal, even to myself, why I wrote the words that I wrote. There is an unknowability about the processes that went into my making and the history of my experiences that cannot be so easily teased apart; and I would venture to say that the same is true as to your responses, as readers, to what I cite above. This black-box of the phenotype does not mean, however, that we should step outside of it (as if we could) and fall back on the general truisms of human nature and human life cycles. Mystery is at the heart, I maintain, of literature, stemming as it does from the evolved, undirected processes that have led to the ceaseless assembly-disassembly-reassembly of unique phenotypes.

The one valid approach is to try and match such evolved obfuscation with a lyrical choice of words on the telling of the narratives. For authors who can be considered more elemental than others (Homer, Shakespeare, Hardy, Emily Brontë) it is the poetry that carries the day, despite the truisms; and for authors who recognize the subjective chaos of being in a world of individuals (Beckett, Joyce, Woolf) the poetry is an added bonus that turns reality into the sublime.

But that's just my subjective phenotype talking!

Notes

1. The research for this chapter and my forthcoming book *Nurture! Nurture! Nurture! A Biological Explanation of a Sense of Free Will* has been pursued with the generous award of an Emeritus Fellowship of the Leverhulme Trust, UK.

2. Albert-Laszlo Barabasi, *Linked: The New Science of Networks* (Cambridge, MA: Perseus Publishing, 2002).

3. Steven Pinker, *The Blank Slate: The Modern Denial of Human Nature* (London: Allen Lane, 2002).

4. Matt Ridley, *Nature via Nurture: Genes, Experience and What Makes Us Human* (London: Fourth Estate, 2003).

5. Susan Oyama, *Evolution's Eye: A Systems View of the Biology–Culture Divide* (Durham, NC and London: Duke University Press, 2000).

6. G. A. Dover, *Dear Mr Darwin: Letters on the Evolution of Life and Human Nature* (London: Weidenfeld & Nicolson, 2000).

7. D. J. Weatherall, 'Phenotype–Genotype Relationships in Monogenic Disease: Lessons from the Thalassaemias', *Nature Reviews Genetics*, 2 (2001), pp. 245–55.

8. Pinker, *The Blank Slate*, pp. 380–90

9. Hilary Rose and Steven Rose (eds), *Alas, Poor Darwin: Arguments Against Evolutionary Psychology* (New York: Harmony Books, 2000).

10. G. A. Dover, *Nurture! Nurture! Nurture!: A Biological Explanation of a Sense of Free Will* (forthcoming 2006).

11. G. A. Dover, 'Don's Delight', *Guardian*, 20 April 1999.

III What has biology got to do with
     imagination?

5   The biology of the imagination: how the brain can both play with truth and survive a predator[1]

Simon Baron-Cohen

In what sense might something as intrinsically human as the imagination be biological? How could the products of the imagination – a novel, a painting, a sonata, a theory – be thought of as the result of biological matter? After all, such artefacts are what *culture* is made of. So why invoke biology? In this essay, I will argue that the *content* of the imagination is of course determined more by culture than biology. But the *capacity* to imagine owes more to biology than culture.

Let's start with a few definitional issues. What do we mean by 'imagination'? I do not mean mere imagery, though clearly the imagination may depend on the manipulation of imagery. Imagery is usually the product of one of the five senses (though it can also be generated without any sensory input at all, from the mere act of thinking or dreaming). Imagery typically comprises a *mental representation* of a state of affairs in the outside, physical world. I don't want to put you off from reading this chapter by littering it with jargon, so let's just think of a mental representation as a picture in your head. That is what we are going to be calling an image, but that is not the same as imagination. Consider why not.

When we create a visual image of a specific object in our mind, the image as a picture of the object has a more or less *truthful* relationship to that object or outside state of affairs. If the image is a good, faithful, representation, it depicts the object or state of affairs accurately in all its detail. So, mental images typically have 'truth relationships' to the outside world. Of course, to create imagery in the first place depends on having the relevant 'hardware'. To create a photo, one needs a camera. To create a mental image, one needs a sense organ hooked up to a brain. An eye can do the trick, since the retina contains receptors that can code both position and colour in sufficient detail for the brain to which it is hooked up to create an accurate image. But in the absence of an eye, clearly an ear or a finger can do the trick too. With your ear, you can create an image of where that owl might be. With your finger, you can create an image of where your car-keys are.

Imagery may be necessary for human imagination. It has been suggested that all the products of the imagination are derived from imagery, following some transformation of the basic imagery. For example, Rutgers' psychologist Alan Leslie, when he worked in London in the 1980s, proposed that imagination essentially involves three steps. First, take what he called a 'primary' representation (which, as we have already established, is an image that has truth relations to the outside world). Then make a *copy* of this primary representation (Leslie calls this copy a 'second-order' representation). Finally, one can then introduce some *change* to this second-order representation, playing with its truth relationships to the outside world without jeopardizing the important truth relationships that the original, primary representation needs to preserve. For Leslie, when you use your imagination, you leave your primary representation untouched (for important evolutionary reasons that we will come on to), but once you have a photocopy of this (as it were), you can do pretty much anything you like with it.[2]

Let's make this more concrete. Your eye looks at a fish. This causes your brain to form a visual image of a fish. So far, your primary representation 'fish' still has accurate truth relations with the outside world. The real fish has fins, eyes and gills, and so does your image of the fish. Or your eye looks at a woman, and this causes your brain to form a visual image of the woman. Now you not only have a primary representation of a fish, but you also have a primary representation of a woman. This image, like the one of the fish, is also *truthful*. The woman you looked at has long hair and an alluring smile, and so does your primary representation of the woman.

In Leslie's important theory, to create such images or primary representations, the only hardware needed is a visual system that starts with an eye and ends in the visual cortex of the brain. But recall that that is only the first of his three steps. To move beyond imagery to imagination, to progress to steps two and three, one now needs an extra, special neurological mechanism. This extra mechanism can take each of the two primary representations (fish, and woman), and make *copies* of them. Whereas our brain previously just had two primary representations, it now has two second-order representations as well. So that was step two accomplished.

Finally, enter step three. This same special mechanism can now introduce *modifications* to the second-order representations at whim. It can, for example, *delete* some features on each of these second-order representations. Let's delete the head of the fish and delete the legs of the woman. And while we're at it, let's delete her long hair. Clearly these second-order representations are no longer *veridical*, that is, they no longer refer to anything in the outside world truthfully. But that's precisely the point. The brain is there as an evolved organ to represent what is going on in the outside world veridically. If there's a lion out there, the brain needs to know the image created by the visual system is accurate, so it can take the necessary action (fight or flight). But the human brain (while not wishing to sacrifice this important survival function of imagery) can be ratcheted up to do more than just represent the outside world veridically, and modifying second-order representations opens up a world of new possibilities. It allows the brain to think about the possible, the hypothetical, about currently untrue states of affairs.

Of course, *deleting* features from second-order representations is just the beginning of the set of possible changes that this mechanism can introduce. Another sort of change might be to *add* features to second-order representations that the primary representations from which they were derived never had. For example, adding snakes to the image of the woman. Or another kind of change this important mechanism can introduce is to *fuse* two second-order representations together. Just bolt them together to see what this would make. For example, the mechanism can combine the modified second-order representations, to produce the intriguing image of a woman with a fish's tail and with snakes coming out of her head. We can even give this newly formed second-order representation a name (mermaid).

Whereas any animal with a sense organ and a brain attached to it can produce an image (or a primary representation), there is a lively debate about whether any animals other than humans can produce second-order representations.[3] Alan Leslie called the mechanism that can do steps two and three the 'meta-representational capacity' and he argued persuasively that this mechanism lies at the heart of the development of pretend play, and the human ability to mind-read.

Regarding pretend play, it has long been recognized that human infants from age 9–14 months begin to pretend. For example, they may pretend an object has features it does not have (e.g., pretending a toy tea-cup is hot). Notice what is going on here. The infant brain has *added* a feature to the representation of the object that the object does not in reality possess. Or the infant may pretend the object has an identity it does not have (e.g., pretending a toy tea-cup has liquid in it). Or the infant may pretend one object is another (e.g., pretending a toy brick is a tea-cup, seen when the child puts the brick to a doll's lips, as if to offer her a drink). Such 'object-substitution', or playful manipulation of an object's features or identity, can take place *safely* if these modifications are made to second-order representations.

'Safely' in what sense? In the sense that the developing infant brain needs to keep track of what objects are really like in the real world. The brain needs to be able to distinguish between representations of objects that have some claim to be truthful (my eye tells my brain this object is a fish) from those representations that have no claim to being true (I imagine a creature called a mermaid). If the infant brain was introducing such modifications to the primary representations themselves, it would no longer be able to sort out what was real and what was not. This could lead to the infant ending up seriously confused or even deluded about the nature of objects (do fish have women's heads?). It could also lead the brain to fail to distinguish a real threat (this is a lion) from an imagined threat (this is a pretend lion). The brain has paid for itself in evolution, not by wreaking havoc with the veracity of primary representations, but by quarantining the truth relationships of primary representations.

Primary representations have the evolutionary function of representing the world faithfully, in order to build up a knowledge base of what the world is *really* like. Change your primary representations and you risk jeopardizing the quality and reliability of your knowledge base, your database of what reality consists of. Leslie's important insight was that we know normal infants are not confused by pretend play. They do not for a moment believe the pretend tea-cup really is hot. They *know* that it is not, because their primary representation (tea-cup = cold) has been left untouched. And this is only possible because of step two above. By making a *copy* of the primary represent-ation this has, in Leslie's chilling phrase, 'quarantined' the truth. In the second-order representation, none of the usual truth relationships need apply. The pretend tea-cup can be hot even while the real tea-cup is cold. The primary and second-order representations are divorced and can have different functions. The function of a second-order rep-resentation is to allow the brain to manipulate truth in an infinite number of ways, to explore possible rather than real states of affairs. Pretend play does not just allow you to play. It allows you to 'imagine' hypothetical worlds, arguably a prerequisite for the serious enterprise of planning and engineering, as well as art or science.

In what sense might a meta-representational capacity be essential for mind-reading? Let's define mind-reading as the ability to put your-self in someone else's shoes, to imagine the other person's thoughts and feelings.[4] Leslie's deeply interesting argument is that when you mind-read, you again need to quarantine your primary represent-ations. Here's how his argument goes. Just as your mental picture of a fish has 'truth relations' to a real fish in the outside world, so a belief, or a sentence, has truth relations to real events in the outside world. Thus, 'John is having an affair with his colleague' is a primary repre-sentation of a state of affairs, and is true if John is indeed having an affair with his colleague. But when we mind-read, we again take the primary representation (step one), *copy* it so that it becomes a second-order representation (step two), and can then, if we wish, *add* a prefix (step three) that completely changes its truth relations with the outside world.

Thus, we can take the primary representation 'John is having an affair with his colleague' (step one). We can copy it to produce an iden-tical version – 'John is having an affair with his colleague' – except this version is tagged as being a copy or a second-order representation (step two). Finally, we can add a prefix such as 'Mary believes that' to the second-order representation to end up with 'Mary believes that "John is having an affair with his colleague"' (step three).

Such second-order representations have unique logical properties, an insight that Leslie borrowed from the standard views in philosophy of mind. They have, to use the jargon, referential opacity. 'I pretend that "this tea-cup is hot"' is true if I pretend this, irrespective of whether the tea-cup really is hot. 'Mary believes that "John is having an affair with his colleague"' is true if Mary believes it, irrespective of whether John really is having an affair. According to Leslie, and I think he is right, when we mind-read (just as when we use imagination), we employ such second-order representations. I can maintain my own knowledge base (John is not having an affair) while representing someone else's different (possibly false) belief (Mary believes he is). I can maintain my own realistic, true perception of the outside world (this is a lion) while representing possible and imaginary creatures (a lion with two heads). To mind-read, or to imagine the world from someone else's different perspective, one has to switch from one's own primary representations (what one takes to be true of the world) to someone else's representation (what *they* take to be true of the world, even if this could be untrue). Arguably, empathy, dialogue and relationships are all impossible without such an ability to switch between our primary and our second-order representations.

So, what has all this got to do with the original question of whether the capacity for human imagination is, at its core, biological? For Leslie, the capacity for meta-representation involves a special module in the brain, which humans have and that possibly no other species possesses. In the vast majority of the population, this module functions well. It can be seen in the normal 14-month-old infant, who can introduce pretence into their play; in the normal four-year-old child, who can employ mind-reading in their relationships and thus appreciate different points of view; or in the adult novelist, who can imagine all sorts of scenarios that exist nowhere except in her own imagination, and in the imagination of her reader.

But sometimes this module can fail to develop in the normal way. A child might be *delayed* in developing this special piece of hardware: meta-representation. The consequence would be that they find it hard to mind-read others. This appears to be the case in children with Asperger Syndrome. They have degrees of difficulty with mind-reading.[5] Or they may never develop meta-representation, such that they are effectively 'mind-blind'. This appears to be the case in children with severe or extreme (classic) autism. Given that classic autism and Asperger Syndrome are both sub-groups of what is today recognized as the 'autistic spectrum', and that this spectrum appears to be caused by *genetic* factors affecting brain development, the inference from this is that the capacity for meta-representation itself may depend on genes that can build the relevant brain structures that allow us to imagine other people's worlds.

What are the consequences for people on the autistic spectrum, and for our understanding of the role of biology in human imagination? Children with severe or classic autism may end up with an exclusive interest in the real world, with no interest at all either in mind-reading, pretending, or fiction. They may enjoy making patterns with real objects, or watching how real objects behave, but not even spare a thought for how someone else might be feeling or what they might be thinking, or understand why a mermaid or a unicorn is a fun idea. Children with Asperger Syndrome may manage to mind-read to some extent, after a delay in developing this skill. But their delay may mean they still find empathy challenging even in adulthood. They may show a preference for factual reading material over fiction, or for documentaries over fictional films, perhaps because the hardware in their brain that functions to form primary representations and understanding of the real world of physical objects is more highly developed than the meta-representational hardware in their brain that functions to represent possible states of mind.

Since the disability that comprises classic autism is biological in origin, children with autism are offering us a big clue about the biological basis of the imagination. Of course, when the meta-representational hardware develops normally, biology has done its job. From then on, the *content* of our imagination, whether we imagine an angry god or a school of wizardry, a mermaid or a devil, owes more to our specific culture than to biology. But the capacity to imagine depends on genes that build brains with a very specific kind of mechanism – one that we take for granted whenever we form relationships or fantasize.

Notes

1. I am grateful for the support of the Medical Research Council, UK, and to the organizers of and other participants in the symposium on 'Literature, Science and Human Nature' for stimulating this discussion.
2. A. M. Leslie, 'Pretense and Representation: The Origins of "Theory of Mind"', *Psychological Review*, 94 (1987), pp. 412–26.
3. Josef Perner, *Understanding the Representational Mind* (Cambridge, MA: MIT Press, 1991).
4. See Simon Baron-Cohen, *Mindblindness: An Essay on Autism and Theory of Mind* (Cambridge, MA and London: MIT Press, 1995).
5. See Simon Baron-Cohen, *The Essential Difference: Men, Women and the Extreme Male Brain* (London: Allen Lane, 2003).

6 Biology and imagination: the role of culture
Catherine Belsey

One substance

Recent scientific advances have gone a long way to reunite what centuries of dualism had put asunder. The human mind, they indicate, is continuous with the body after all. People, we now know, are inescapably rooted in biology as products of evolution.

As a cultural critic, I am convinced that the humanities disciplines do well to take account of these discoveries. The days of the free-floating consciousness as the determinant of human nature are gone, and yet this recognition does not necessarily diminish the importance of human culture. On the contrary, it locates and grounds the processes by which we come to make sense of our world. For example, developments in neurobiology, by showing that thoughts, perceptions and feelings have a material existence, which can be mapped as the actions and interactions of neurons, give those supremely human experiences more weight, not less. The scientific challenge to Cartesian mind–body dualism takes ideas out of a nebulous realm of unearthly abstraction and gives them substance, the same substance as the materiality of the organisms that human beings also are. Culture – as the virtual world produced by the physiology of the brain – is real.

Functionalism

Because, however, cultural critics have unduly neglected these advances, because, in other words, most of the new developments have been defined and explained from the point of view of the scientists, there tends to be a serious downside to the story so far. If I have an anxiety about the inferences that are widely drawn from the science of human behaviour, it concerns the functionalist framework in which the implications of the research are so often understood and presented. Darwin's theory of natural selection is made to do more work than Darwin himself might have thought possible. Natural selection is taken to imply that every existing human emotional, behavioural and cognitive capability *functions* to confer reproductive advantage.

This reductive point of view is widely apparent in current popular science, and nowhere more so than in evolutionary psychology, which ascribes the habits of our own society to an unchanging human nature conjecturally shared with the hunter-gatherers who distinguished themselves from our hominid ancestors about 100,000 years ago. But evolutionary psychologists are not alone in this belief. On the contrary, they share with many biologists and neurobiologists the belief that human beings display the same basic inclinations and tendencies at all times and in all places, and this is because, like the rest of the animal kingdom, we are ultimately nothing more than survival machines, driven by the imperative to live long enough to disseminate our genes. According to one influential biologist: 'Widely distributed traits are usually adaptive, and their existence accords with the first principles of evolution by natural selection. It is further true that by and large people behave in their daily lives as though somehow guided, whether consciously or unconsciously, by these first principles.'[1]

Culture in this account tends to come out, predictably enough, as expressive or instrumental, no more than a component of the 'distinctive design that allows us to survive, prosper, and perpetuate our lineages'.[2] Thus, an eye for beauty helps in the quest for the fittest mate;[3] the religious impulse is heritable, conferring the selective advantage of belonging to a powerful group; ethical conviction stems from biology, because cooperative individuals live longer.[4] Why do we have a sense of self, V. S. Ramachandran wonders; after all, this 'must have evolved through natural selection to enhance survival'. And he answers that self-consciousness functions to ensure that we recognize the otherness of other people, since 'we primates are intensely social creatures'.[5] It follows from the survival value of all these universal characteristics that individual and cultural distinctions are merely the local manifestation of organically rooted drives we share with all other human beings. The new sciences of human behaviour and cognition, it is claimed, 'expose the psychological unity of our species beneath the superficial differences of physical appearance and parochial culture'.[6] This unity is understood in terms of innate responses to the environment, genetically based. Surface diversity masks the sameness of a biologically determined, foundational human nature – and suddenly science has become the new metaphysics. Perhaps because they feel impelled to contest creation theory, the scientists seek a single alternative key to all mythologies, and natural selection takes the place of God as the one origin and explanation of all living things.

Without abandoning the unquestioned insights of this work, we could now perhaps afford to move towards a more nuanced view of culture. We might, for example, allow that once it has evolved, as it did some 40,000 years ago, culture has its own history and its own imperatives, which interact with biology in ways that are not always harmonious, driven by a survival mechanism, or instrumental in conferring reproductive advantage. The Darwinian story of natural selection, invoked to explain changes in species over millions of years, does not do justice, I cannot help thinking, to a certain waywardness in the short history of human beings, who so commonly fail to act in accordance with the values that ought logically to motivate the organisms they are. Instead, people often seem to risk their own health, well-being and even their lives in the pursuit, at best, of a utopian world and, at worst, of hatred and destruction. Indeed, as the twentieth century so copiously demonstrated, sometimes these two objectives are conflated in political programmes designed to create what their proponents claim are a better alternative to the way things are. And so far, the twenty-first century seems no less dangerously committed to inflicting damage in the name of conviction.

Of course, even the most dedicated Darwinians acknowledge the existence of human waywardness, insofar as the history of the last 100 years has hardly allowed us to forget it. Most notably, whole populations have turned themselves over to social experiments that proved deeply destructive. But one widely held scientific account of Nazism and Stalinism is that they were deviations, deluded precisely to the degree that they flew in the face of human nature. Based on theories that were fundamentally *un*natural, they couldn't work because they failed to take account of human nature as it is.[7]

Conversely, as luck would have it, human nature, left to its own devices, is widely held in popular science to issue in the way of life the West currently holds most dear. According to Edward O. Wilson, whose work has been so influential in this field, 'What really matters to humanity, a primate species well adapted to Darwinian fundamentals in body and soul, are sex, family, work, security, personal expression, entertainment, and spiritual fulfilment.'[8] From this point of view, the values that conform to nature are reducible to self-interest, tempered by cooperation in the community, with the arts for recreation and 'fulfilment', and a commitment to family values. (It should be noted that these family values are often flexible enough to allow a certain amount of extra licence for men, who are able to disseminate more genes in the course of their lives than women.) Conveniently enough, this combination of 'natural' values translates readily into the corporate market by day (especially for men) and a safe suburban home at night (well, most nights, anyway) to provide a relief from all that competing and cooperating, with TV to entertain the heterosexual couple and their offspring in the evenings. Evidently, the whole of evolution has led inexorably to Walton-on-Thames (or possibly Westport, CT). The coincidence between the lessons of natural selection and the aspirations of the stockbroker belt might just give us pause for thought. Human nature, as science and suburbia both interpret it, appears just a little – well – *unimaginative*. Surely our intellectual capabilities can visualize at least the possibility of something more challenging for us than this?

In the mid-twentieth century the influential American sociologist Talcott Parsons appropriated evolutionary theory for a functionalist analysis of social development. Parsons did not mistake culture for biology: his human beings are cultural animals, and the symbol replaces the gene as the basic structural element of cultural change.[9] Instead, his idea was that the development of social life was intelligible by *analogy* with natural selection: societies evolved in the same way as organisms. Parsons anticipated some of the complacency that characterizes so many recent scientific accounts of human nature. According to his social theory, the society that adapts most success-fully to its environment advances along the path of social evolution; all societies encounter problems on this path, but those that succeed in solving them continue to evolve, while others either disintegrate or remain static; success depends on the ability to turn obstacles into contributions to the survival of the society itself.[10] In the long run, every feature of a society is necessary to it: whatever *is* has been selected for its survival value. Social evolution both differentiates and unites. As development requires more and more distinct forms of expertise – law and order, writing for long-distance communication, money to mobilize resources, democratic politics to ensure consent – this differentiation of social practices is countered by an increasing uniformity of identity, norms and social systems. Ultimately, what survives in evolved societies is exactly what has turned out to help the society evolve, *functioning* to preserve its integrity. Conflict is inci-dental and will be resolved; radical challenges must either be incor-porated or fall away.

Parsons singled out America as having evolved further than its European counterparts,[11] and this gratifying account of its own excep-tional character had a marked appeal in America itself. Functionalism as a way of interpreting the world sank deep into intellectual life there. It surfaced in the 1980s in American new historicism, which erroneously attributes its own emphasis on cultural containment to Michel Foucault, and it reappears, equally silently, in a good many of the current scientific accounts of human nature, though this time without the distinction Parsons maintains between natural selection and cultural evolution. Now there is a single determinant of social behaviour, and it is biology itself.

In this new model, mind–body dualism is reversed rather than transformed, as consciousness is said to function on behalf of physi-ology: 'The mind exists for the body, is engaged in telling the story of the body's multifarious events, and uses that story to optimize the life of the organism.' Psychological processes come into being because the body needs them: consciousness 'is a necessity for survival'.[12] Culture can seem to have a limited independence, but in the long run it must be subordinated to nature. Thus, in the book he subtitles *The Unity of Knowledge*, E. O. Wilson promises to synthesize science and the humanities. He concedes that features of culture *may* emerge that reduce Darwinian fitness, but only 'for a time. Culture can indeed run wild for a while.' The clear implication is that this wildness will not last; human beings will be duly reined in to ensure that society continues to function on behalf of biology.[13]

Wilson's own theory of 'gene-culture coevolution' initially sounds as if it might attribute a degree of autonomy to culture. But his examples indicate that culture simply expresses epigenetic rules, so that 'Gene-culture co-evolution is a special extension of the process of evolution by natural selection.' In other words, culture is no more than the instrument of biology.[14] The 'co' in co-evolution turns out to work as follows: genes prescribe rules, but culture helps to determine which genes survive; newly successful genes change the rules, which change the culture; and at this point there is a degree of 'play' in the system, which will be contained in due course. This falls a long way short of any account that allows culture, once it has evolved, a significant contribution to the process of shaping human destiny in all its waywardness.

Imagination

A little ingenuity can find a functionalist explanation of more or less anything. The science of human nature credits imagination itself with survival value. It permits us to hallucinate specific, identifiable satisfactions for our appetites. Imagination also enabled our ancestors to conjure up images of creatures and situations that could do them harm, as well as to visualize unknown places that might be worth the effort of migration.[15] Thanks to imagination, we can empathize with other people, entering vicariously into their perceptions and feelings, and this empathy facilitates the capacity for cooperation that fortifies human groups against predators and natural disasters. We can impro-vise in unforeseen situations,[16] choose between alternative options, and invent new social skills or new technologies.[17] Imagination creates alternatives to the world we know, and comes out in the scientific lit-erature as generally beneficial – as functioning, in fact, to confer advantages.

And it generates stories, which are also functional. Since stories link objects and events in a causal sequence, one evolutionist maintains that narrative as 'the root of human thought' is the supreme outcome of natural selection.[18] Not everyone grants it this much importance, but fiction, known in all human societies, is generally seen as an effect of imagination, and is variously understood as itself adaptive, or the by-product of adaptations. Appropriating a capacity selected for its survival value, imagination gives rise to narratives. These can be instructive, providing heroic role models, and nurturing altruism, by this means promoting the social and moral values that will generate responsible, caring parents.[19] It certainly encourages pair-bonding: a high proportion of narratives are stories of faithful love. Alternatively, fiction names dangers to avoid. Stories also add to the human reper-toire of 'pleasure technologies'.[20] Recounted round the fire and in the mead hall, dramatized in the amphitheatre or on television, stories are just what we need to relax after a hard day's hunting and gathering, defending our territory, or competing and cooperating in the city.

An example

This all makes perfectly good sense, as far as it goes. Can we confirm it from examples? Take *A Midsummer Night's Dream*. Here is a play that pleasurably embodies a world of fantasy, a delightful counterfact-ual realm, filled with sudden, unaccountable love and lyric poetry, a flower that gives rise to irrational passion, a queen who spends the night with a donkey, and a character able to fly round the earth in 40 minutes. Judging from the theatrical history of Shakespeare's play, we wouldn't want to be without the recreational advantages offered by this jubilant demonstration of imagination at work. If we choose, we might also derive instruction from its account of the errors that can attend the courtship rituals leading to pair-bonding. And it includes in its own plot a second fictional work of high comedy in the guise of tragedy, designed to entertain the court itself after a day spent hunting and getting married. The theory seems to work perfectly in this instance.

Or does it? Does *A Midsummer Night's Dream* really support the idea that imagination functions on behalf of biology? Most of the scientists I have read are clear that pretend possibilities are easily decoupled from reality, except among psychotics. In one version fictional worlds come into being in baby-talk, where carers play at peek-a-boo, or 'this little piggy', to the delight of the infant, who gurgles responsively. But even at this stage, the scientist argues, children know the difference between reality and pretence.[21] Stout scientific common sense insists that the capacity to distinguish fact from fiction is a fundamental property of human cognition.[22] Functionalism, of course, requires us to suppose that this distinction is given: the inability to decouple in this way might be 'catastrophic'.[23] True, if the audience of *A Midsummer Night's Dream* waited for the fairies to sort out their love lives, they might be doomed to sterility; supposing you could fly could lead to nasty accidents.

Ironically, however, one of the characters in the play itself tells a rather different story. Theseus does not share the scientific confidence that everyone knows fact from fiction. Instead, Shakespeare's Duke of Athens aligns artists and suitors with psychotics, in order to dismiss the delusions of all three: 'The lunatic, the lover, and the poet / Are of imagination all compact' (*A Midsummer Night's Dream*, 5.1.7–8).[24] The insane see demons where there are none, he says; love is blind to what others recognize as imperfections; and creative writers bring into being what does not exist. In this view, it's not only psychotics who fail to decouple imagination from reality: we are all prone at times to take fantasy for truth. The rational – but entirely non-Darwinian – Theseus wants none of it. In his view, imagination is anything but beneficial. Instead, it invades reality to mislead us into anxieties we could well do without: 'in the night, imagining some fear, / How easy is a bush suppos'd a bear!' (5.1.21–2).

But there seems to be a contradiction here. Surely, we should expect the imaginative and pleasurable play to present the Duke's curmudgeonly dismissal of imagination as misguided, a killjoy view that belies human nature? Strangely, it does not exactly do this. Instead, *A Midsummer Night's Dream* raises a question it does not set out to resolve, quite possibly enhancing the pleasure it offers in the process. It invites its audience to speculate on the question whether imagination constitutes an asset or a liability.

In the play the Duke doesn't have it all his own way. Hippolyta argues that the imaginative delusions of the lovers in the course of this fertility festival of arbitrary and fast-changing relationships deserve to be taken seriously (5.1.23–7). Thanks to the transforming intervention of the magic juice, which realigns the couples, leaving Demetrius still in its power, the lovers can all be married off satisfactorily, and the story moves smoothly to its happy ending. In this respect, Shakespeare's fictional play records an aspect of truth that the most functionalist of the behavioural and cognitive scientists would surely endorse. Romantic love is both powerful and blind; it is like madness; it involves taking an idealizing, imaginative picture of the loved one for real; and by this means it cements the pair-bonding that keeps the parents together to bring up the children.

Imagination, then, as a component of sex, is inclined to be benign, it would appear, precisely to the degree that it *doesn't* get decoupled from reality. The incursion of fantasy into facts is not necessarily pathological. This complicates the scientific model. Suppose we complicate it a bit further. Is imagination always functional? The problem with romantic love is that it is transferable: you can idealize donkeys, the play indicates, or, more dangerously, other people's partners. Supported in our own time by a whole industry of flowers, Valentine cards and candlelit dinners, the romantic delusion, it turns out, continues to have alarmingly interchangeable objects in real life. For some, the pleasure is positively intensified by prohibition: adultery is more sexy because it's forbidden, and not just for men, who are permitted to be more interested in disseminating their genes. As the rising divorce rate indicates, when it comes to sex, imagination can operate either for better or worse.

It is hard to conceive of voluntary human sex without an element of fantasy. Steven Pinker offers a functionalist explanation of adultery: it allows men to have more offspring and women to find better fathers for their children.[25] Conversely, of course, there is also evidence that it can interfere with pair-bonding to a point that may prove damaging for the offspring. But there are cases where the imaginative condition of gratification seems to have no functional value at all. In some instances, it's dressing up in a uniform, or being treated like a baby, or punished like a naughty boy. And here we begin to get into a realm where imagination leads a life of its own. It is difficult to see how getting sexual excitement from domination, or the surrender of power to a person with a whip and leather boots, would help ensure the survival of anyone's genes. Without a high degree of control, S & M can be quite risky. But there is a lot of it about, apparently.

On the basis that both Theseus and Hippolyta have a point, that fantasy might or might not be functional, depending on the context, my own view is that, once it has evolved in human beings, the imagination goes its own way. Rooted in biology in the first instance, the capacity for fantasy takes on a degree of autonomy. It develops a material existence to the degree that it motivates behaviour, and this behaviour may be malign on occasions. The stories imagination generates may not confine themselves to entertainment. At this historical moment, it is apparent that the stories of Jesus and Mohammed respectively far exceed recreation, or even 'spiritual fulfilment'. If the claims made for one are true, the other's must be false, at least at the level of detail. But they indicate the part narratives can play, not only in history but in current international relations. Like love, mythology precisely does not decouple fact from fiction; and in practice stories can be a matter of life and death. The scientists who analyse human nature may not like religion, but if they cannot do better than write it off as delusional, they place current violent confrontations outside the norms of the human nature they set out to define. A foundational theory that cannot account for history is not worth much of our attention.

For better *and* worse?

Towards the end of *A Midsummer Night's Dream* Bottom and his friends perform the tragedy of *Pyramus and Thisbe*. Peter Quince writes the script, based on what he remembers of Ovid from first-year Latin at the grammar school. As a work of art, this play-within-the-play leaves a good deal to be desired, and even the most fumbling modern production can hardly fail to make it funny. Hippolyta understandably finds the performance silly (5.1.207). Now, however, Theseus seems to think better of his earlier scepticism. The actors, he reflects, are amateurs doing what they can to please. After all, 'The best in this kind are but shadows; and the worst are no worse, if imagination amend them' (5.1.208–9). Alongside what these hopeless performers are, we can glimpse what they might be, amending the facts to produce a counterfactual vision that is not quite so silly, despite appearances.

In the course of history, that amending imagination has produced some of the best and the worst of human achievements. For one thing, it drives the development of knowledge, as science produces hypotheses about what we don't already know, opportunities we could explore, diseases we might cure. In addition, it has brought democracies out of dictatorships. But it has also generated social experiments that involved exterminating swathes of the population. Imagination accounts for both art and pornography; or for Shakespeare's play and Peter Quince's. The ability to imagine a better alternative has fuelled both feminism and the oppression of women, who were thought to have caused all the trouble; the same amending imagination generated the civil rights movement, but also apartheid; it impels utopian idealists and suicide bombers. History demonstrates the degree to which counterfactual visions can have material consequences, and we ignore them at our peril.

There is a logical fallacy in the supposition that, because cultural processes register neurologically in the brain, their motivations are always reducible to biological drives. Many cognitive scientists concede this point in theory, but then go on writing and talking as if biological processes are the sole determinants of behaviour. Scientists are not, of course, the only people to be seduced by the dream of a single, metaphysical first cause. Theology gratifies much the same longing to find the one foundational explanation of everything.

But human life might be more intractable than this. The infant human animal may have no imperatives apart from survival, but very soon language and pictures, as the inscription of culture, will open up whole new horizons that will substantially change its world. In *The Prehistory of the Mind* the archaeologist Steven Mithen goes some way to credit language with a degree of independence, while still remaining wedded to natural selection. At this stage he allows it a critical role in differentiating modern humans from their evolutionary predecessors, on the grounds that only language permits the flow of understanding between one specialized domain and another, opening up the possibility of analogical thinking.[26] Five years later he comes to see art as performative, and not merely expressive: a 'cognitive anchor' for fantasies, art helps to construct the cultural script.[27]

Language and pictures enable people to specify what is not present, and in this sense to conjure up in their absence images of objects and events, whether real or imaginary. Meanwhile, the capacity to make demands and concessions in words confers a power to alter the world in material ways. Moreover, the acquisition of language introduces difference into the continuity of the world, and thereby bars us irreversibly from any purely organic, instinctual existence. By these means, culture alters those who internalize it, defining what seems obvious, constraining what appears possible. Children, most people agree, have to *learn* to interact, to love, to think clearly and make sound choices. These processes of socialization and education help us to realize our capabilities, but they also change us.

The expansion of the options that culture confers is characteristically human, and it creates the possibility of a *lack* of fit between the organisms we are and the narratives that *make us* their own. In my view, it is the friction between the two that we need to think about, if we really want to know what drives the organisms-in-culture, the imagining, storytelling, reasoning, choosing, amending, and potentially destructive beings that little human animals grow up to become.

Here, too, the science of human nature concedes the point in one sense. Obviously, medicine has interfered with evolution; science itself opens up a range of choices, so that we can modify nature, not just submit to it; rationality can conflict with older, more instinctive elements of the brain. Moreover, there may develop a mismatch between adaptive traits, such as aggression, for example, or storing up fat in case of famine, and the current conditions in which these traits may become dysfunctional. But my contention is not simply that specific elements in culture might from time to time come into conflict with the imperatives of nature. Instead, it is that once the human animal takes on an identity conferred by (any) culture, the possibility of conflict between the organism and social values is endemic.

Dissatisfaction

The friction that inhabits fully human organisms-in-culture generates a restlessness that surely accounts better than a bland functionalism for human behaviour in the course of the centuries. European thought has not generally been drawn to functionalism, or to any version of the complacent conviction that whatever there is must have survival value. Instead, thanks, perhaps, to our own divided history, we have tended to interpret the world in terms of struggle – between capital and labour, or power and resistance, or morality and desire. From this perspective, civilization is above all a location of *dis*-contents, and these discontents have motivated exploration of the options, discovery, the imperative to know more, often at the cost of personal comfort, health or security.

Moreover, serious science itself is not necessarily functionalist either. The biologist Gabriel Dover has written a series of witty and instructive letters to Charles Darwin, deploring the uses to which his theory of natural selection is now so reductively put. In reply, Darwin takes a lively interest in recent biology, which traces modifications to a range of factors, including chance. Natural selection is one component in the process of change, and it works to contain the excesses random modifications can bring about. At the same time, some things survive despite their inefficiencies: the eye, for example, works well enough, but it could have been different. As it is, the eye wastes energy and is more complex than it need be.[28] Biological organisms are not engineered; they function and survive despite themselves. Dover's essay in this volume develops his biological case against a universal human nature: scientifically, he argues, the unceasing generation of differences cannot be ignored, and the reduction of diversity to fundamental sameness misrepresents what biology reveals.

Oddly enough, the popular scientists often seem to acknowledge a difference between what they say and what they do, or to recognize the restlessness that motivates their own work, even if their theories contradict it. One of the most persuasive accounts of the way neurobiology illuminates culture must be Antonio Damasio's *Looking for Spinoza*. Damasio argues that feelings are functional. Grounded in the body, they seek equilibrium for the organism, homeostasis. Feeling well, as he defines it, means lying on a beach at 78 degrees F in a slight breeze.[29] Social institutions are developed, he goes on to argue, to secure the benefits of equilibrium for the greatest number: to maximize life, liberty and the pursuit of happiness. Paradoxically, however, Damasio's hero in this book is Spinoza, an outcast and a rebel, who lived in relative poverty as a result of his refusal to conform to the norms of his society. Spinoza spent his life contesting the dominant assumptions of Cartesian philosophy as well as organized religion, and his work was banned then and for many years afterwards.

To make his argument hang together, Damasio is obliged to argue that Spinoza's iconoclasm must have made him feel contented. We shall never know how Spinoza himself really felt about it, but there was no lying on beaches at 78 degrees F for him. And not as much as there could be, indeed, for the intellectually adventurous Damasio himself.

Early in the book the author of *Looking for Spinoza* describes the beginning of his own quest for his hero: he went out for a walk in a hurricane, despite the best advice of the hotel doorman, in search of the house where Spinoza had lived in the Hague. Not much equilibrium there, then, but something very revealing, just the same. If there is such a thing as human nature, it is sometimes impelled to seek more than homeostasis. Like explorers, detectives, artists, neuroscientists, evolutionary psychologists, cultural critics and people who read books about human nature, many of us seem to be driven, often against the interests of an easy life, to know more than we do already. We stay up late, or get up early, to read, or write, or test a theory to destruction. A certain discontent inhabits the organisms-in-culture that we are: a dissatisfaction with the present state of things, an imperative to do better, or to change the world; above all, a capacity to dream up alternatives to the way things are.

What permits us to do this is culture, as the place where meanings circulate and clash. In the first instance, language enables us to define and distinguish. Education consists above all of expanding our vocabularies, so that we can think a wider range of thoughts, differentiate more sharply between positions, argue more cogently for one as opposed to another. And in the second place, imagination enables us to suppose that things might be other than they are. But this amending capability does not always produce the most virtuous outcomes: it also leads to conflict and conquest, domination and destruction.

At its best, the science of human nature concedes that its own functionalism gives no more than an ultimate account of human nature. Sometimes, however, the ultimate can seem a long way from the empirical and the immediate of most lives. Sadly, much human behaviour comes across as deeply dysfunctional, and if the scientists *are* right, the implication of that must be that what we learn from our different cultures has been powerful enough to override the best interests of the organism – time and again.

In my view, the biology that constitutes human beings always interacts with the relatively autonomous culture their evolved brains make possible, and culture too exercises determinations. If there is such a thing as human nature it *is* that conjunction: an organism equipped by biology to learn from culture how to act either for or against the imperatives of biology itself.

Notes

1. Edward O. Wilson, *Consilience: The Unity of Knowledge* (London: Little, Brown, 1998), p. 190.

2. Steven Pinker, *The Blank Slate: The Modern Denial of Human Nature* (London: Allen Lane, 2002), p. 60.

3. Pinker, *The Blank Slate*, p. 53.

4. Wilson, *Consilience*, p. 281.

5. Vilanayur S. Ramachandran, *The Emerging Mind: The Reith Lectures 2003* (London: Profile, 2003), pp. 121, 124.

6. Pinker, *The Blank Slate*, p. xi.

7. Antonio Damasio, *Looking for Spinoza: Joy, Sorrow, and the Feeling Brain* (London: Heinemann, 2003), p. 168; Pinker, *The Blank Slate*, pp. 169–70.

8. Wilson, *Consilience*, pp. 299–300.

9. Talcott Parsons, *The Evolution of Societies*, ed. Jackson Toby (Englewood Cliffs, NJ: Prentice-Hall, 1977), pp. 25–6.

10. Talcott Parsons, 'Evolutionary Universals in Society', *The Talcott Parsons Reader*, ed. Bryan S. Turner (Oxford: Blackwell, 1999), pp. 157–81.

11. Parsons, *The Evolution of Societies*, pp. 182–214.

12. Damasio, *Looking for Spinoza*, p. 207.

13. Wilson, *Consilience*, p. 174.

14. Wilson, *Consilience*, p. 140.

15. Steven Mithen, 'The Evolution of Imagination: An Archaeological Perspective', *SubStance*, 30 (2001), p. 41.

16. John Tooby and Leda Cosmides, 'Does Beauty Build Adapted Minds? Toward an Evolutionary Theory of Aesthetics, Fiction and the Arts', *SubStance*, 30 (2001), p. 19.

17. Pinker, *The Blank Slate*, p. 406.

18. Mark Turner, *The Literary Mind* (Oxford: Oxford University Press, 1996), p. 12.

19. Paul Hernadi, 'Literature and Evolution', *SubStance*, 30 (2001), pp. 55–71.

20. Pinker, *The Blank Slate*, p. 405.

21. Ellen Dissanayake, 'Becoming *Homo Aestheticus*: Sources of Aesthetic Imagination in Mother–Infant Interactions', *SubStance*, 30 (2001), pp. 85–103.

22. Pinker, *The Blank Slate*, p. 215.

23. Tooby and Cosmides, 'Does Beauty Build Adapted Minds?', p. 20.

24. William Shakespeare, *A Midsummer Night's Dream*, ed. Harold F. Brooks (London: Methuen, 1979). All references are to this edition.

25. Pinker, *The Blank Slate*, p. 252.

26. Steven Mithen, *The Prehistory of the Mind: A Search for the Origins of Art, Religion and Science* (London: Thames and Hudson, 1996), pp. 185–94, 214–15.

27. Mithen, 'The Evolution of Imagination', pp. 50–1.

28. Gabriel A. Dover, *Dear Mr Darwin: Letters on the Evolution of Life and Human Nature* (London: Weidenfeld & Nicolson, 2000).

29. Damasio, *Looking for Spinoza*, pp. 83–4.

7 The limits of imagination

Rita Carter

Human imagination, we humans imagine, lifts us above other creatures because it allows us to spring free of the here and now. A mental excursion to Narnia or Brobdingnag, Middle Earth, Discworld or Lyra's Oxford suggests that it is practically unbounded; that in our mind's eye we can travel beyond the range of memory, defy the laws of nature and slip free from the limits of biology.

If this were so – if our minds really could float free of the material world – there would be an aspect of each of us that is transcendent. It would justify human claims to be 'special' among animals.

When human imagination is scrutinized, however, its limitations become apparent. Our flights of fancy are slotted into existing conceptual templates – notions of time, space and embodiment – which are physically encoded in our bodies. These force us to see both the 'real' world, and the worlds we dream up, in a particular way. If our bodies (and particularly our brains) are structured normally we will never imagine anything that we could not, in theory at least, experience in reality.

We cannot, for example, imagine an eight-dimensional world. Mathematicians tell us that we probably exist in one, and we may believe them, but we will never *imagine* it because our bodies extend into only four dimensions. Nor can we imagine a true abstraction – infinity, or idealized justice – because our symbols are grounded in sensation. And the only sensations we can imagine are familiar ones. Try as you might, you will never be able to imagine 'seeing' as a bat 'sees', or 'hearing' like a whale.

Imagination seems at first to be quite distinct from perception of the external world – the sort of here and now awareness we assume we share with all sentient beings. Whereas I feel that I can make anything I like of my fantasy world, my perception of 'reality' is non-negotiable. I see a blue mug on the desk in front of me because it is there, and it has intrinsic qualities which make it look blue. I am inclined to assume my cat sees it too, in much the same way.

People's visual perceptions are usually so alike that they are for most intents and purposes identical. If a group of people were to be presented with the light waves that are bouncing off my blue mug, for example, it's unlikely that one of them would exclaim 'There's a hippopotamus!' while another protests: 'Rubbish! It's clearly a carrot.' All of them would probably say that they saw a blue mug. Close interrogation might reveal that one of them sees a slightly greener-blue mug than another, but the differences would generally be unimportant. Not only that, but all the people would see the blue mug in the same way: which would not be an x-ray view, or a view of it as seen by a heat-detecting camera, or a view of it as seen through an electron microscope.

Yet perception is itself largely imagination. Our close consensus about what's 'out there' obscures the fact that what each of us sees is not 'given' but individually constructed. Perception is the end result of a creative brain process which can be likened (up to a point) to product assembly in a factory. At one end raw materials – light rays, sound waves, molecules and vibrations – come in via our sensory organs, and at the other end there emerge the finished products – thoughts, emotions and sensations. The reason that the external world appears similar to us all is not because there is only one way to see it, but because the assembly lines in our brains are so alike that we all manufacture it in a similar way.

Our human consensus encompasses not just our perceptions of concrete objects, but also the way we see things in a more abstract sense, right up to sophisticated issues of social conduct. Despite the fact that human beings grow up in vastly different environments, practically all of them agree that food is good, a roaring tiger is frightening, a smile is more inviting than a frown; that pain is nasty and murder wrong. This common view is an evolved way of seeing things. It is the one that best equips us to survive. If our survival needs were different, our view would be different too. The mug on my desk looks blue to me because my visual apparatus has evolved to distinguish a wide range of colours, presumably because this gave my ancestors some advantage in foraging for food. The light waves from the mug are those that generally give me a 'blue' experience, but they do not do that *necessarily*. Despite my casual assumption that my cat sees things much as I do, it is actually very unlikely that the mug is giving him a 'blue' experience comparable to mine, because his eyes and brain do not process light waves in the same way as mine. In this, as in many other things (the fun potential of a mouse on the bed, for example) the cat and I do not share a common view of reality. We see things differently because we do not *make* the same of it. Human physiology dictates that we see things as we do, just as a cat's physical form and function dictates that it sees mice as delicious playthings.

In order to make anything of the stimuli from which we construct experience we need to interpret them, using pre-existing concepts about the world. By concepts I mean any sort of knowledge, prejudice or disposition: memories, beliefs, ideas, even the species-specific distribution of cones in the retina that cause me to see blue where my cat probably sees grey.

Concepts, in this sense, are both mental processes and physical states. Recalling a personal memory, for example, involves the activation of a distinct (though constantly changing) neural firing pattern within a distributed system – a process. If you call up the last sight you had of your mother, the brain areas which will be activated include the hippocampus, temporal cortex and parts of the visual cortex. This combined activity is the neural correlate of the image you see in your mind's eye. But the memory also has a physical existence, of a sort, even when it is not being recalled. This is because the neural firing pattern correlating with a memory is largely preserved from recall to recall by physical linkages between the relevant cells. Each time a particular neuronal firing pattern occurs the cells involved form stronger bonds between their axons and dendrites. In the case of long-term memories (the ones you 'relive' in recollection, or hold as known facts) the neurons involved are located in the association areas in the temporal lobes. Although it requires systemic activation – that is, other areas, such as the hippocampus or prefrontal cortex, need to be active in order for these patterns to fire up – long-term memories can be triggered just by stimulating a cortical 'storage' area with an electrode. If you had a sensitive enough microscope and knew what to look for, you might even be able to discern the shape of a memory, woven like a cobweb in the dense tissue of the cortex.

Before a concept can inform perception, it has to be switched on. That is, the neurons in the pattern which encodes it need to be firing. If they are firing rapidly (more than 40 times a second) they become conscious, but even when they are firing at a lower rate, and are not therefore actually 'in mind', they can still influence behaviour. Certain concepts are more or less permanently ticking over at this subconscious level throughout our waking life. If we lost them we would lose our ability to 'make' anything of the world at all.

To see a visual image, for example, we need an operative concept of space. You might think that such an idea is unnecessary because space is simply *there* – you don't have to invent it in your head before you can be aware of it. But this is not so. Our brains are primed to be aware of space – the parietal lobes contain a sort of spatial template closely associated with the body maps which grant us awareness of our bodies. Because the idea of space is thus physically encoded in our brains, it is vulnerable to physical injury. Certain types of brain damage produce a condition known as neglect, in which the individual loses awareness of one or another 'chunk' of space and, with it, awareness of any objects within that space. The most common type of neglect involves the loss of one half of the visual field, but sometimes it is 'near' space (the area immediately surrounding the person's body) that is lost, or 'reaching space' (the area within the stretch of their limbs).

A person's ignorance of a 'neglected' area is more profound than if they were blinded to it – it is not just that they can't see it, they don't realize it is there *to be* seen. Neglect is probably not caused by *erasure* of the concept of the neglected area of space, but by damage to the attention system which prevents people from activating the neurons in which the notion is encoded. Several studies of affected persons have shown that – even in their mind's eye – the lost area cannot be accessed. For example, when a patient with left-side neglect was asked to describe an imagined walk from the south coast of England to the Scottish Highlands, she named only the towns in the east on the way up, and only those in the west on the way down.[1] Our concept of space is only useful so long as we can tell one bit from another. We have to know that 'here' has a particular relationship to 'there', rather than just being different. For that we need to have a mental concept of our bodies which we can place within our mental space. Only when we have placed ourselves firmly within it do we, literally, know where we are. If we did not have this idealized body it would be rather like having a map of a strange town – useless without an arrow saying 'you are here'.

Our body concept has to be kept 'switched on', at least at a low level, in order for us to use our (actual) body appropriately. It remains 'on' by being constantly stimulated by incoming sensory information. Some of this comes from outside. When we walk, for example, the pressure on our feet tells us how our bodies are interacting with the floor. But most of the information is proprioception – a constant stream of messages coming from our joints, muscles, and the movement detectors in our middle ear. This information impacts on the conceptual body and changes it from moment to moment, keeping our inner sense of our body lined up with what is happening to the real thing. The concept, though, is always just a little ahead of the reality. It takes the information coming in 'now' and uses it to construct a model of how our body will be a split second later. This is just the time it takes for the concept to become conscious, should it do so. Therefore, when we become conscious of our body it seems that we are conscious of it in 'real time'. As we feel our weight shifting from the pushing foot to the stepping one in our walk, for example, our body concept is altered to match what we expect when the stepping foot hits the ground. Most of the time the prediction is so good that the real experience is more or less indistinguishable from our idea of it. Indeed, we don't have to take account of the external information at all, because we have already incorporated its effect into our concept, which ticks along, getting us about the place, without becoming active enough to be conscious.

However, if we put our foot down a hole and produce a sensory experience that clashes with the predicted concept of how our body is supposed to be at that moment, the concept has momentarily failed and needs very quickly to be rearranged. To do that the brain has to extract as much 'real' information as possible, in order to construct a more realistic internal model. At such times the neural representation of our body – caught in the act of incorporating new information into itself – becomes excessively active and flares into consciousness. Once the model is happily reharmonized with the outside world it slips back into tickover mode.

The distinction between our conceptual body and the real thing is manifest most clearly in sleeping dreams or waking 'out of the body' experiences. In sleep, the signals from the body that normally keep the two things – concept and reality – closely yoked are blocked off, so our dream body is just our concept, uninformed by proprioception or external stimuli. Hence our experience of it can float free of the flesh.

The most basic feature of our body concept is its boundary – where it begins and ends. Although the conceptual boundary is plastic in that, as in dreams, it can detach itself from the physical boundary, it is not easily breachable. We have an extremely strong concept of our bodies as whole, integral, undamaged entities, and it doesn't adapt easily to change. When someone loses a body part through amputation, therefore, it is common for them to continue to feel it, in the phenomenon known as phantom limb. When people with this condition say that they can 'feel' their lost arm, what they are actually conscious of is the concept of that arm – which is still securely lodged in their brain.

Conversely, if the concept itself is partly lost, consciousness of the matching body part will be lost too. Stroke patients who suffer damage to the body map in their brain become partially paralyzed, either because the signal pathways between their real body and their conceptual one are broken, or because part of the body concept is itself wiped out. In the latter case, patients seem to lose not only feeling and movement in the affected 'real' body area, but also the sense of owning it.

It moves beyond their body consciousness, becoming an object 'out there' rather than an integral part of their selves.

The idea of our body – and the related concept of space – might seem to be the most deeply 'plumbed-in' concept we have. But in fact there is another concept that is even more taken for granted by humans: that of time. Like space, it seems absurd to think of time as an idea. It seems just to *be*. But if that were the case – if time proceeded at its stately pace without any conceptual input – it would pass at the same pace for each of us, whatever our circumstances and whatever the condition of our brains. And that is not the case. Even in common experience we find that time does not proceed smoothly. Anyone who has ever been physically involved in or witnessed a traumatic event will know the sensation of time slowing down. Conversely, when we are tired and struggling to do the things that need to be done in the day, time seems to fly past us, leaving us constantly in its wake.

The notion of flowing time is encoded in a neural circuit in the brain fuelled by the neurotransmitter dopamine. Each 'loop' of activity takes, on average, one-tenth of a second to complete, and events registered by the brain within the duration of a single loop are experienced as a single occurrence. If the activity in the brain's time loop slows down, therefore, events get compressed in subjective time, so everything seems to go faster.

Such variations in subjective time are not usually great enough to affect our ability to function, but if the timing mechanisms in the brain are severely disrupted by illness the effect can be disastrous. People with Parkinson's disease commonly have a completely different idea of time to everyone else, because their internal clock is slowed down by their insufficiency of dopamine. If you ask most people to say – starting at a certain moment – when they think a minute has passed, their answer, typically, will be to say 'now' after about 35–40 seconds. Parkinsons patients (without medication) are likely to opt for a far longer duration.

The concept of time can be disrupted by damage to any part of the neural loop that comprises the brain's internal 'clock'. One 66-year-old man, for example, found one day as he drove to work that the other traffic seemed to be rushing towards him at terrific speed. And he simultaneously felt that his own car seemed to be going unusually quickly. Even when he slowed down to walking pace it seemed to be hurtling along too fast for him to control it. He found that he couldn't watch TV because things happened too quickly for him to keep up with them, and he seemed to be perpetually tired. When doctors tried the '60-second' test on him, he waited nearly five minutes before saying 'time up'. A medical examination revealed that the cause of the man's problems was a growth in his prefrontal cortex.[2]

Subjective time may even stop altogether. Damage to the basal ganglia and/or frontal lobes sometimes produces a state known as catatonia, in which people may become 'frozen', like living statues. Some such affected persons have been paralyzed in mid-action, their hand outstretched as though to reach for something, or contorted into strange postures which they may hold – despite what would normally be severe discomfort – for days at a time. Although they do not appear to be conscious during this time, some patients have later reported that they had memories of it, but that their recollections lacked any sense of passing time and that their consciousness was utterly still and devoid of possibilities. A sense of timelessness – though starkly different from that of catatonia in that it seems *full* of possibility rather than empty – is also reported by people in meditation or trance.

At the other end of the scale, people whose brains are suddenly thrust into overdrive experience an acceleration in subjective time, with a corresponding deceleration of events in the outside world. This is what happens when excitatory chemicals flood the brain during terrifying experiences like accidents, or thrilling ones like a first parachute jump. Suddenly consciousness becomes very clear, with each tiny change in the environment noted and considered. Even when the experience is awful, it delivers an overwhelming sense of being alive.

The sharpening of consciousness experienced when the brain is excited gives a hint of how our concept of time dictates what we are aware of. Our normal idea of the present moment is equivalent to one of the 'temporal packets' or 'ticks' of the internal clock – around one-tenth to one-fifth of a second. Each tick is the time it takes for the current to run around a loop of dopamine-producing cells in the brain. All the information we process during that time-window is experienced as happening simultaneously. This is probably, at our human scale, the optimum 'size' of the time packet which is available for us to make sense of things. It means that when a cup falls off the table next to us we see the object hit the floor at the same time as we hear the crash, even though – as light travels faster than sound – there is actually a minuscule gap between the visual stimulus entering our brain and the auditory one. It also allows us to 'smear' time, fleshing out the subjective moment by squashing into it all the events that fall into a particular time packet.

The drawback is that each of our moments is slightly blurred. When we watch the beating of a fly's wings, we cannot see each individual flap because several of them happen in each of our time windows. The result is that we see a fuzzy haze rather than a clear outline of a moving wing. If our subjective concept of time was more fine-grained, allowing us to split each moment into many more parts, we would see things more clearly. That we have not evolved to do so is probably because such clear-sightedness would burden us with more information than we need. After all, what advantage is there to seeing the individual beats of a fly's wing? The things we need to discriminate most clearly are those that happen in seconds (animals moving or, today, cars bearing down on us) – not milliseconds. Just as there is no need for us to experience all the visual details that our brains detect unconsciously, time experience is most usefully cast in relatively broad brushstrokes. Only when we are faced with a life-threatening situation, or one which is wildly exciting, can we afford to ignore everything in the past and future and concentrate on the present moment. And when that happens our brains oblige by breaking the moment into more parts so each one can be separately scrutinized and dealt with.

In addition to the fundamental concepts that mould our experience, we each have a huge database of individual memories which give shape and colour to everything we perceive and imagine. Each one begins as a tiny 'seed' of sensory experience. The concept of a dog to a baby, for instance, is probably no more than a particular sensation – the waft of hot doggy breath or a big moving shape. But over time it becomes more and more complex. The doggy sensation becomes 'furry thing that goes woof!' and then grows to be hugely elaborate, incorporating ideas about different breeds of dog, the history of dogs, the biological characteristics of the genus *canidae* and so on. It may also be linked to other concepts: dog-days and dog-fights, doggie-bags and dogged people, dog-lilies and dog-ends, so that when any one of these ideas crops up it drags with it a whole host of associations.

Most of the things that happen to us get forgotten almost as soon as they happen. But some of them stick in the mind as memories, or act on existing concepts to alter them. The *ugh* experience of eating a bitter fruit may not itself be remembered, but it might leave a permanent mark by changing or elaborating an existing idea about apples.

The concepts formed by memorizing certain experiences and conjoining them with related ones provide a massive database of knowledge that can be brought to bear on new experiences, and therefore affect behaviour. Take, say, a memory of being bitten by a dog. It will be bound in with existing memories of dogs – of hairy bodies, wet noses, Rover, and so on. Any experience that occurs thereafter which 'hooks' on to these peripheral memories will therefore also bring to mind – consciously or not – the memory of the bite. So a new experience of a dog will be attended by a certain degree of caution.

There is, however, a limit to the usefulness of such knowledge so long as it can only be accessed by a reminder that is purely sensory (the experience of a wet nose). The concept that 'dogs can bite' remains locked away until it is needed – right here, right now. It cannot be used to predict what might happen in the future, or what might be happening to someone else, someplace else. In order to make that concept of a dog biting readily available, on tap, it has to be encoded in some way that makes it, so to speak, 'portable'. The meaning derived from the real event (*ouch!*) has to be extracted from the memory and put into a mental vehicle that caters for all events which contain that meaning. In other words, it needs to be symbolized.

The symbols used by humans to transport such experiences are words. Language – the structure in which words are embedded – can itself be considered as a concept. Rather like the body maps which need only to be 'filled in' by physical exploration, the structure of language seems to be mapped in. You can actually see the parts of the brain where this language 'instinct' is lodged. Wernicke's and Broca's areas make a discernable bulge (in right handers) along the side of the left hemisphere. When these areas become active, around the age of two, children start to use language to communicate but – perhaps more importantly – they also start to use it to structure their inner world. Language provides a scaffold for thoughts which, without it, would be amorphous and fleeting. It allows us to crystallize ideas, to link them to other notions, to encode them in a way that makes them retrievable on demand, to project into the future, and to string thoughts together in a rational and communicable train.

Once an experience is attached to and encapsulated in words, therefore, much of the sensory, 're-liveable' nature of that experience falls away, because we now have a way of conveying information (dogs can bite) and thus making it 'useable', without having to recall the experience itself. We may even seem to forget the experience and be left with just an idea.

If ideas could be totally divorced from bodily experience we would be capable of imagining pure abstractions. When we think about things like dogs biting, without invoking a mental image of such a thing, it seems that this is what we are doing. This is not the case, however. Rather, it seems that everything we can imagine has some physical 'presence' for us. Every word and every thought is connected to a bodily experience.

Bodily elements are easy to grasp when we think in images. After all, an image is a sensation. And even the faintest of imagined images is created, in part at least, by a replay of some previous experience, or a juxtaposition of several such experiences. Similarly, the meaning that we discern in music is conveyed through its sensuality – a musical score means nothing if we cannot translate it into imagined sound.

But what about, say, a chair? We don't visualize a chair every time we say the word – sentences are not like those dumbed-down TV documentaries where every word of the script has to be accompanied by the matching image. So it is easy to think that the word 'chair' is used instead of a sensation, that the 'felt' meaning of the object has been transferred into a symbol. That is not the case.

We learn new concepts by linking them to ones we already have. These conglomerations form categories – living things, for example, may be one category, man-made things another. And categories are organized like Russian dolls. 'Furniture', for example, may be nested within the larger category of 'man-made things', and 'chairs' may be nested inside the 'furniture' category. Types of chairs – a throne, say – will in turn be nested within the 'chairs' category, and 'the Bishop's throne' within the 'throne' module, which is itself inside the 'chairs' category.

If each category is as 'real' as any other, a child might first learn about their grandmother's rocking chair and then learn to 'nest it' within the larger category of chair, working from the bottom up. Or in different circumstances they might first learn that there are objects called 'furniture' and then learn to discriminate chairs. If the brain was working as a detached learning machine, it really wouldn't matter which concept came first.

But it does matter. The 'chair'-level categories (other examples are 'tree', as opposed to 'plant' or 'oak tree', or 'horse' as opposed to 'animal' or 'carthorse') are, in crucial ways, more 'basic' to the brain. They are learnt first. They enter language before the others, and are identified faster by nearly everyone. They seem to comprise our 'default' picture of the world.[3]

One reason for this seems to be that this is the highest categorical level at which you, and I, and everyone else who uses 'chair', find common meaning through our bodies. I can't imagine sitting in 'grandmother's rocking-chair' if my grandmother never had one. Or rather, to do so I would first have to create an imaginary rocking chair, imagine it belonging to Grandma, then imagine myself sitting in it, which is quite a conceptual effort. And I can't intuitively know what to do with 'furniture', because 'furniture' could be anything from a bed to a bookcase. But say 'chair' to anyone and they know how their body would interact with it, because you put your backside on the seat and bend your knees to interact (normally) with *every* sort of chair. Each member of the furniture category, in contrast, requires a different sort of motor action: lying down (if it's a bed), opening a door (if it's a cupboard), placing things on it (if it's a table), and so on. It therefore seems that the perfect example of any conceptual category is not the one that best encompasses all the others, as you might suppose, but rather the one that best exemplifies the way that everything in the category is physically experienced.

The way that we store and retrieve concepts also reveals their links to physical movement. Word knowledge is 'stored' in the language areas of the brain. But when a person is asked to think of a particular word, it does not just 'pop up' from the word bank. Brain-imaging studies show that the word's meaning is 'gathered' from widespread brain areas, including those that process sensations and plan movements in response to the object represented by that word.

Strange as it may seem, it is impossible even to *think* of a word without moving. Language-based thought (and most thought is contained in language) is accompanied by the beginnings of the motor actions required to articulate the words aloud. The area of the brain most closely concerned with speech production, Broca's area, is essentially a movement area – it triggers activity in the muscles that allows the lips, tongue and throat to produce sounds. When people read, even quietly, alone, to and for themselves, this area produces tiny contractions of those muscles, even if we long ago learnt to stop our lips moving. And the amount of muscular activity is not related so much to the complexity of the words that are being uttered, but to the amount of movement implied by their *meaning*. Reading a list of verbs produces more motor activity than does reading a list of passive words.

Furthermore, the movement is not limited to Broca's area. One study found that when people saw words relating to tools – things that they would expect to pick up and use – the part of the brain which would normally plan the body movements required to deploy the screwdriver or the hammer became active, as though the tool was right there in front of the person, just begging to be put to use.[4] Symbols, then, may be partially abstracted – that is, taken away from the bodily sensations associated with them – but they are never cut off entirely from physical experience. The brain keeps them connected through its elaborate feedback system, by which concepts track back to the sensations and actions associated with them, and actions and sensations constantly form and update their symbols.

The brain's creation of 'action plans' with regard to objects may be what it takes to make the objects meaningful to us, or perhaps even to make them visible, or imaginable. From this it would follow that if an object has no potential for physical interaction we simply could not form an idea of it. We may very well be blind to many aspects of the world in which we live, simply because we do not create an intention to interact with them.

It is impossible, of course, to point to things we cannot sense. We can *think* of such things, as we can think about the possibility of other dimensions, but even in imagination we cannot experience them. There may be surfaces we fail to see because we cannot stand on, move across or place things on them. The surface of a bank of hot air in the sky, for example, may be clearly visible to a gull, looking to hitch itself a ride on a rising current. The fact that it is not clearly visible to humans is not necessarily just a matter of not having evolved the right sensory equipment – experienced glider pilots can 'read' the sky in a way that others cannot, just as a fisherman sees subtle changes in the sea which escape landlubbers. Rather, we do not have the concept required to recognize these things, in the same way that a person with neglect does not have the idea of the part of space to which they are blind. The only sort of awareness we can have of these 'hidden' things is what we can derive from existing, 'near-to' concepts, much as a blind man might get an idea of 'red' by thinking of the rich tone of a bassoon. It is only an approximation, though. To be conscious of the real thing you would have to construct an action schema that involved preparing your wings to glide on the surface. And that is beyond normal human imagination.

What, though, of *abnormal* imagination? When people diverge from the consensual view of reality we regard them as either mentally deranged or gifted visionaries, depending on whether their behaviour is socially acceptable or disruptive. The hallucinations, delusions and bizarre behaviour associated with psychoses were once deemed to be supernatural in origin – the work of God or the devil – and in some cultures they still are.

Eccentric ways of seeing the world occur when a person's brain puts together the raw materials of perception in an unusual way, due to some physical abnormality. The physical difference may be gross – a (literal) hole in the head, like poor Phineas Gage,[5] or microscopic, a matter of molecular changes in a handful of brain cells. Such abnormalities occur for all sorts of reasons. The person's brain may have been damaged by injury or disease or affected by some abnormality in another part of the body. It may have developed in an unusual way due to a rare genetic constitution, been changed by some extraordinary event, moulded by weird cultural conditioning, or temporarily altered by a drug. Whatever the historical reason, the *immediate* cause of a person 'losing touch with reality' is an abnormality in the structure or functioning of the nervous system.

Given that the normal way of seeing things evolved because it best equipped us to survive, one would expect any departure from the norm to be dysfunctional. But this is not always the case; sometimes abnormal biology creates a view that enriches us all. Einstein, for example, 'saw' the space–time manifold in an act of imagination that preceded the laborious process of working out the mathematics that confirmed the intuition. One reason for his genius was probably the missing groove in his brain which allowed information to flow between neurons that would otherwise be separated. Several great artists did their best work during periods of mania, a condition associated with changes in the neurochemistry of the brain, and deliberate alteration of brain function through drugs inspired the Romantic poets to some of their most celebrated work. So, although human imagination may be limited by biology – biology is pliable. One day, perhaps, we will learn how to alter it in such a way as to create any experience we desire.

Notes

1. J. C. Marshall, P. Halligan and I. H. Robertson, 'Contemporary Theories of Unilateral Neglect: A Critical Review', in *Unilateral Neglect: Clinical and Experimental Studies* (Hove: Erlbaum, 1993), pp. 311–29.

2. F. Binkofski and R. Block, 'Accelerated Time Experience after Left Frontal Cortex Lesion', *Neurocase*, 2 (1996), pp. 485–93.

3. Mark L. Johnson, 'Embodied Reason', in *Perspectives on Embodiment: The Intersections of Nature and Culture*, ed. Gail Weiss and Honi Haber (New York and London: Routledge, 1999), pp. 81–102.

4. T. J. Grabowski and A. H. Damasio, 'Premotor and Prefrontal Correlates of Category-Related Lexical Retrieval', *Neuroimage*, 7 (1998), pp. 232–43.

5. Phineas Gage was a nineteenth-century railway worker who suffered a massive injury to the prefrontal lobes of his brain in a freak accident. Before the accident he was a model citizen, but after it he became a wastrel and drunkard. His case is regarded as a classic example of how a person's personality seems to be dependent on their physical form.

IV   Do we need a theory of human nature
      to tell us how to act?

8 Human nature or human difference?

Ania Loomba

> Is there any value in the fact of a philosopher's having started off from a scientific experiment or from a 'literary' experience? That is to say, which philosophy is more 'realistic' – that which starts from the 'exact' sciences or that which starts from 'literature', i.e. from the observation of man in so far as he is intellectually active and not just a 'mechanical part of nature'?
>
> Antonio Gramsci[1]

For the symposium from which this volume emerged, speakers were asked to reflect on C. P. Snow's assertion that literature and science had stopped speaking to one another and become two distinct cultures, but they were asked to do so by meditating on the subject of 'human nature'. It is striking that ideas about 'human nature' have come to represent the space of mutual incomprehension, the division between literature and science. In posing the question this way, the suggestion is that all scientists think alike about human nature, searching for universal answers in biology, while literary critics, departing from their earlier belief in the eternal transcultural and transhistorical human nature made visible by great literature, have been beguiled by postmodernists, postcolonialists, feminists and queer critics so that they now think in terms of different, contingent natures shaped by society rather than inner essence or genes. But is it really true that literature and science suggest different answers to similar questions about human nature? Or indeed that science and literature do not ask, and do not in fact expect to ask, similar questions about human nature or indeed the human condition?

In setting up the debate between 'science' versus 'literature' we simplify the issues at stake by ignoring or underplaying the role of those scientists who do not believe that human nature or behaviour can be explained by our genes, or indeed the ways in which humanists and scientists have historically collaborated both in propping up racist or sexist notions of human nature, and in debunking and critiquing them. Antonio Gramsci's words remind us that the 'reality' about human beings will always include more than their 'natural' being, but also that the positions from which we start – scientific or literary inquiry – cannot entirely account for any conclusions we might arrive at concerning human nature. In what follows I will suggest that the crucial debates about human nature are not about the differences *between* sciences and the humanities. Rather, the debates about human nature encode competing visions of human society, and on each side we can line up scientists, humanists and literary figures. For it is the case that whenever we offer opinions about human nature, we are actually speaking about human societies, and more importantly, about human difference.

Recently I heard Richard Lewontin, one of the foremost geneticists today, speak about our haste to believe in science '*in spite* of the patent absurdity of some of its constructs, *in spite* of its failure to fulfil many of its extravagant promises of health and life'.[2] Urging his audience to be sceptical about the 'genomania' that has increasingly begun to sweep our world, Lewontin argued that genetic science will not unlock the mysteries of human existence, because 'life is not a controlled experiment'. Human behaviour is far more complex and variable than a set of genetic prescriptions will allow. Moreover, genetic science is often misrepresented in the media by being oversimplified for the general public; at other times, many supposedly scientific conclusions about the behavioural implications of our genetic makeup are often derived in a completely unscientific way. Asked, inevitably, about the possible genetic coding for homosexuality, Lewontin answered by referring, tongue-in-cheek, to what one of his colleagues had called the 'knitting gene'. This knitting gene, his colleague had suggested, must be a jumping gene, for until the Industrial Revolution in Europe, when home knitting was the norm, most knitters were men. After the Industrial Revolution, when mechanization of garment manufacture made home knitting less profitable, men stopped knitting and women constituted most of the home-knitters. Thus, the gene must have jumped and become a female gene. Lewontin was of course suggesting that just as it is absurd to draw conclusions about the genetic makeup of knitters from the simple observation of the largest number of those who knit, so too it is unscientific to draw conclusions about the genetic coding for homosexuality from commonsensical assumptions and observations of gay people around us. Lewontin urges us to remember that correlation is not causation; his argument is that many of the 'scientific' conclusions that make headlines and dazzle the general public are simply bad science, or science watered down for public consumption, reduced to a set of clichés which usually confirm rather than challenge ideas and social values that are already normative.

Of course, the possibility of a genetic base for homosexuality has also been entertained by advocates for gay rights because, as Alan Sinfield points out, it is widely supposed that if a certain behaviour is genetically dictated then it cannot be understood as abberational or perverse, and nor can it be regarded as a matter of individual culpability or choice.[3] Thus the comparison between homosexuality and ethnicity or race is appealing because the rights of ethnic minorities have come to be more widely established than those of gays. But this is a contested point within the queer movement because it takes away the right of individuals to choose or vary their sexual desires, and also because race and ethnicity have progressively been uncoupled from their supposed base in biology, which had been established in the heyday of imperialism by racist science.

These contestations alert us to the fact that the question of a genetic basis for human behaviour is, at its base, a *political* one. Today, it is a curious fact that so many of the conclusions that the 'hard-wired' lobby comes to are simply a reiteration of older stereotypes or hierarchies that have in fact been effectively discredited by intellectuals as well as social activists. That male aggression and jealousy are natural, or blacks less intelligent and inherently more violent, or that women are less equipped for higher mathematics or science than men (as the President of Harvard University has very recently informed us) – are these really 'facts' to be discovered or simply established prejudices legitimized in the name of scientific research?[4] Is it not striking that they are being reasserted now, when the racist biology of the colonial era has been so thoroughly discredited, and when feminists have similarly questioned the patriarchal basis of so much scientific research? As a whole spate of articles following the Summers episode reiterated, feminists do not deny that there may be differences between men and women; they simply contest the patriarchal (and rather unvarying) meanings assigned to these differences. These meanings are defined by social power, but they are paraded as scientific truth and as the truth about human (or male and female) nature.

Any debate on human nature must simultaneously discuss human culture and social formations for, as the biological anthropologist Jonathan Marks points out in his book *What It Means To Be 98% Chimpanzee*, it is impossible to conceive of one without the other. Pointing to studies that show that primates are genetically more diverse than humans, he asks: 'How, then, are humans able to make sense of their place in the social world, to know what groups they belong to, and who else does, if they don't have much biological diversity to guide them, as other animals do?' The answer, he says, is that 'Cultural diversity is the true evolutionary hallmark of humans, and it serves the purpose . . . of telling us who we are, of identifying ourselves in the social universe . . . group hostilities inevitably lie in the social, political and economic realms, and not in the biological'.[5] However, as the sad history of colonialism and racist science reminds us, such political and historical hostilities have been routinely pathologized, and this tendency continues today under new forms. A recent *New York Times* report entitled 'Hard-wired for Prejudice? Experts Examine Human Responses to Outsiders' quotes one Dr Steven Spenser as concluding that 'Thinking bad things about people in another group . . . makes people feel better about their own group "which then makes them feel better about themselves" '.[6] Thus we can explain away our intolerance and our stereotyping of others as arising out of a need to protect ourselves from danger, and from what the report called 'the mind's tendency to make sense of the world by categorizing and simplifying'.

To categorize and sort out human behaviour may in fact be a universal human tendency, but as Geoffrey C. Bowker and Susan Leigh

Star point out in their book *Sorting Things Out*, it is not a biological but a political act; they narrate the following story:

> In an episode of *The X-Files*, a television show devoted to FBI investigations of the paranormal, federal agents Mulder and Scully investigated a spate of murders of psychics of all stamps: palm readers, astrologers, and so forth. The plot unfolded thusly: The murderer would get his fortune read or astrological chart done, and then brutally slay the fortune-teller. It emerged during the show that the reason for these visits was that he wanted to understand what he was doing and why he was doing it, and he thought psychics could help him understand his urges to kill people. Only one psychic, an insurance salesman with the ability to scry the future, was able to predict his murderous attacks and recognize the criminal. When finally the murderer met this psychic, he burst out into his impassioned pleas for an explanation of what he was doing. 'Why am I compelled to kill all these people,' the salesman responded in a world-weary tone such as one might take with a slow child: 'Don't you get it, son? You're a homicidal maniac.' The maniac was delighted with this answer. He then proceeds to try and kill again. . . . The story is powerful and funny because it reminds us, ironically, that a classification is not of itself an explanation. All we understand at the end of the scene is that the maniac now has a label that others, and he himself, can apply to his behavior. Although the classification does not provide psychological depth, it does tie the person into an infrastructure – into a set of work practices, beliefs, narratives, and organizational routines around the notion of 'serial killer'. Classification does indeed have its consequences – perceived as real, it has real effect.[7]

Thus Bowker and Star urge us to understand the ways in which this work of classification happens – in the sciences, in the social sciences, in the humanities, and indeed in everyday life. Who makes categories? Who decides the lines between them? Who institutionalizes these categories such that they become received knowledge? Further, because over time we learn to take the classifications for granted, they get naturalized, and then exert a huge power over us.

These questions are also crucial in thinking about the idea of 'human nature' – a category that claims to be above categories, and to include all human beings. But in practice, as Marks demonstrates in some detail, 'human nature' has never really meant *everyone's* nature; rather it is a concept that has been developed through ideas of difference or inequality. For ancient Greeks, humanity was equivalent to the ability to speak Greek, and 'barbarism' was the attribute of non-Greek-speaking peoples. But, as Irad Malkin shows, the Greeks were aware that those whom they called barbarian, 'the non-Greek civilizations of the Near East, such as Egypt and Babylon, were richer, more powerful, and far more ancient'.[8] For this reason the difference between human and barbarian in the Greek world was not equivalent to the binary oppositions between Europeans and non-Europeans that were later established, largely in the wake of colonial contact.

European imperialism hardened and reduced attitudes towards outsiders to a set of manageable stereotypes. Of course in practice, because colonialism also brought enormous numbers of people from different parts of the world into contact with one another, these stereotypes were always unstable, and never able to contain the complex reality of what Mary Louise Pratt has called 'contact zones'.[9] Marks observes that Hobbes, Locke and Rousseau all needed the idea of primitive man to develop their otherwise completely divergent notions of human nature. Hobbes believed that humans were naturally aggressive while Rousseau believed that they were noble, but both assumed that

(1) there was a kernel of nature to be revealed beneath the layers of culture; and (2) the way to access it was through the most cultureless societies known, supposedly those of the Amerindians.

And thus the study of human nature became the study of Indians. And through the nineteenth century, students of Indian languages would imagine they were studying something primitive and similar to the primordial or 'natural' language of man; and students of Indian society would imagine they were studying the basic, and most rudimentary, manifestations of the social instinct in humans.[10]

From the very beginning of modern colonial contact it was assumed that supposedly universal attributes about 'human nature' could be identified by studying people without 'culture'; Marks traces how, in this search for 'human nature', the Native Americans were replaced by Australian Aborigines, and then by the !Kung San of the Kalahari desert. By the 1980s, while

> sociobiologists continued to represent the !Kung San as surrogates for 'early man', living the Edenic life . . . Ethnohistorians [traced their] history of contact with pastoralists, European traders, colonialism, and economic exploitation: far from being pristine and standing outside of world history, the !Kung San were very much products of that very world history. Their lifeways constituted revelations not about 'people' in general, not human nature per se but about *them* in particular and them in relation to other people.[11]

In 1992, Richard Lee, co-organizer of the !Kung San project at Harvard, believed that he was wrong in trying to locate 'the human condition' among the !Kung San; rather:

> The human condition is about poverty, injustice, exploitation, war, suffering. To seek the human condition one must go . . . to the barrios, shantytowns, and palatial mansions of Rio, Lima, and Mexico City, where massive inequalities of wealth and power have produced fabulous abundance for some and misery for most . . .[12]

By the 1990s, Marks shows, after all the colonized people of the world had been studied (and many decimated), there was a new surrogate for 'natural man' – the chimpanzee.

Thus the search for a universal 'human nature' has had a very particular social and political history, inseparable from colonialism. In some ways, the replacement of 'natural man' by the chimpanzee has been foreshadowed throughout colonial history, right from the early days of European contact with non-Europeans. Edward Topsell's *The Historie of Four-Footed Beastes*, published in 1607, pictured a baboon, a 'Satyre', and an 'Aegopithecus', with erect genitals, and located such creatures in Ethiopia, and among 'Moors' and in India. The book suggests that 'Men that have low and flat Nostrils are libidinous as Apes that attempt women, and having thick lips the upper hanging over the nether, they are deemed fools, like the lips of Asses and Apes.'[13] While Topsell does not use the word 'race', he lays the basis of a comparison between apes and black people. By 1634, this connection was made explicit by Thomas Herbert, who had no doubt that Africans 'have no better predecessors than monkeys'.[14]

Thus the association of savages with primordial nature was never an index of their innocence and goodness, but functioned as a marker of their inferiority. This was true not just of sub-Saharan Africans and others who were regarded as bestial but also those who, like the early Americans, were seen as embodiments of the 'noble savage', as was pointed out in the seventeenth century by the French humanist Michel de Montaigne. In his essay, 'Of the Cannibals', which was appropriated by Shakespeare's play *The Tempest*, Montaigne suggests that the inhabitants of the newly discovered 'boundless country' (i.e. the 'New World') are like the fruits of Nature, among whom there is

> no sort of traffic, no knowledge of letters, no science of numbers, no name for a magistrate or for political superiority, no custom of servitude, no riches or poverty, no contracts, no successions, no partitions, no occupations but leisure ones, no care for any but common kinship, no clothes, no agriculture, no metal, no use of wine or wheat . . . They are not fighting for the conquest of new lands, for they still enjoy that natural abundance that provides them without toil and trouble with all things necessary in such profusion that they have no wish to enlarge their boundaries . . .[15]

In the eyes of most of his countrymen, says Montaigne, these people are inferior because they are culture-less. While Montaigne suggests that he himself does not think of the cannibals as inferior in any way, the idea of a natural man is always poised to turn from an idealized vision to a demonized one. Thus in *The Tempest*, Prospero's island inspires in the old courtier Gonzalo a vision of primordial bliss that is shaped by Montaigne's essay. Gonzalo declares that if he had 'plantation' of the isle he would not admit 'traffic' (trade), or 'magistrate' (law), or letters; there would be no riches or poverty or 'use of service', all men would be 'idle', all women 'innocent and pure', and nature would bring forth 'all abundance/To feed my innocent people'.[16]

Gonzalo's vision of a culture-less and equal society still envisions him as ruler and colonist over the natives. Moreover, the vision is framed by the exploitation and torture of the real native of the island, Caliban, who is represented in the play as neither innocent nor innately good but as someone who is naturally inferior, someone who, being culture-less, needs to be ruled by Europeans. Prospero alleges that Caliban is 'a born devil, on whose nature/Nurture can never stick' (4.1.188–9). He is a 'natural' man who simply cannot be civilized or assimilated into culture. Prospero's daughter Miranda suggests otherwise, pointing out that Caliban does learn his master's language. But, she says, there is a quality in him which makes him irreducibly different: 'thy vile race . . . had that in't which good natures/Could not abide to be with' (1.2.360–2). Thus she reverses Montaigne's terms by associating 'good natures' with Europeans, and Caliban with an uncivilized but far from innocent monstrous 'race'.

The Tempest foreshadows the way in which the division between 'culture' and 'nature' was to operate in colonial history. The entire colonial debate about indigenous people was to centre around whether and how natural man might be civilized. This in turn shaped colonial policies towards various indigenous people and the degree to which they, and other colonized peoples, could be brought into a Europeanized mainstream. In yet another play, Shakespeare shows how marginalized people believe themselves to be somewhat less than human, and in striving to embody the dominant notion of humanity, lose their way in the world. Essentially, this is the story Shakespeare narrates in *Othello*, a play that is both a fantasy of interracial love, and a nightmare of racial hatred and male violence.[17] Consider the curious fact that until recently, Anglo-American critics tended to disregard or underplay the question of racial difference in this play, casting it as a story about universal and universally valid manifestations of human nature – violent male jealousy on the one hand, and pure un-understandable evil on the other. Hence most readings of the play sugested that Othello's jealousy is to be understood as a *universal* male attribute and Iago's hatred is, as Samuel Taylor Coleridge put it, simply 'motiveless malignity'. By these accounts, both Othello and Iago should be read as just universal men, rather than black and white men. Now, such a move is apparently benign, but what gets left out if we read both Othello and Iago as attributes of universal human nature is Shakespeare's powerful depiction of racism and misogyny. What also gets ignored, and thus silently naturalized, is the view, prevalent in Shakespeare's time and actually articulated in the play, that it is *black* men who are especially prone to jealousy and violence.

But in fact Shakespeare goes out of his way to draw attention to Othello's colour and race, which are the butt of Iago's vitriolic commentary. 'A black ram', Iago tells Brabanzio, is 'tupping your white ewe'; there is something unnatural, he suggests, in Desdemona's flouting of the established social hierarchies of 'clime, complexion and degree' to marry a black man. Desdemona's act indicates 'Foul disproportions, thoughts unnatural!' (3.3.235–8). Notice that 'Clime, complexion and degree' – location, skin colour, and class – are seen to add up to 'nature' itself. What Iago thinks is human nature, Shakespeare tells us, is composed of several interlocking social and cultural factors. Shakespeare also goes out of his way to engage with the prevalent notion of his time that both blacks and Muslims were given to unnatural sexual and domestic practices, were highly emotional and even irrational, and prone to anger and jealousy. In Giraldi Cinthio's *Gli Hecatommithi*, from which Shakespeare took the story of the unhappy marriage of a Moor and a Venetian lady, Desdemona tells her husband, 'you Moors are so hot by nature that any little thing moves you to anger and revenge'. Shakespeare has his Desdemona counter this stereotype; when Emilia asks her, 'Is he not jealous?' she replies, 'Who he? I think the sun where he was born/Drew all such humours from him' (3.4.28–30). But despite initially seeming different from other Moors, Othello ultimately embodies the stereotype of Moorish lust and violence. He becomes a jealous, murderous husband of a Christian lady. Why does he do so? Is he returning to his essential nature? Is he hard-wired, fated to play out the script of wife-murder? Is he genetically programmed as a *man*, or as a *Moor*?

Iago himself does not believe Othello is the jealous type: 'The Moor . . . Is of a constant, loving, noble nature', he says (2.1.287–8).

But this 'nature', he believes, can be transformed so that it begins to conform to the stereotype of the jealous Turk. What is significant is the process by which this happens. At the beginning of the play Brabanzio has already cautioned Othello: 'Look to her, Moor, if thou has eyes to see./She has deceived her father, and may thee' (1.3.292–3). Iago practically echoes these lines: 'She did deceive her father, marrying you,/And when she seemed to shake and fear your looks/She loved them most' (3.3.210–12). He warns Othello against 'the green-eyed monster' who consumes those men who expect fidelity from their wives, whereas 'That cuckold lives in bliss/Who, certain of his fate, loves not his wronger' (171–2). Women, in his opinion, are capable of the most unnatural acts such as loving black men, and the greatest fickleness, by ceasing to love them. By asking Othello to acknowledge this, he both questions Othello's humanity and appeals to his manhood: 'Are you a man?', he asks. 'Have you a soul or sense?' (3.3.378); or again, 'Would you bear your fortune like a man?'; 'Good sir, be a man', 'Marry patience;/Or I shall say you are all in all in spleen/And nothing of a man' (4.1.61, 65, 87–9). The more he questions Othello's humanity, the more he suggests that Othello should be outraged by Desdemona's behaviour and assert his masculine power over her. Promising to kill Cassio, he begs Othello to 'let her live', although Othello has not until that time even hinted at the idea of killing Desdemona.

For Othello, the only way to yoke together the otherwise contradictory experiences of being black and a man is to embrace the discourse of female duplicity. Whereas he had once believed that he had no cause for jealousy because Desdemona 'had eyes and chose me', he now echoes Iago:

O curse of marriage,
That we can call these delicate creatures ours
And not their appetites. (3.3.267–74)

There run two common threads in Brabanzio's, Iago's and Othello's beliefs – first, that this match is unusual, 'unnatural', and therefore especially fragile, and second, that women are inconstant and deceitful. Whether Othello imbibes these beliefs from Iago, or Iago only plays upon what Othello already believes, the point is that for all of them, male jealousy in this play is seen to be born out of the tensions of both race and gender relations in Venice. Othello is a victim of racial beliefs precisely as he becomes an agent of misogynist ones. Ideologies, the play tells us, only work because they are not entirely external to us. Stories about female nature, the nature of blacks or Muslims, about what it means to be human are powerful precisely because they persuade us and shape the course of our actions. Competing theories of human nature already exist around us. Some of them are more powerfully circulated than others, others may appeal more to us as individuals because they confirm our place in the world or help us challenge it. If we want to choose which ones we will believe, we must begin by looking at their constructedness, see how they are put together, by whom and why.

I deliberately chose to make this point via *Othello*, not only because its story reflects so powerfully upon the question of whether human nature is constructed or natural, but also because the critical history of the play reminds us that when we *erase* the question of social difference we can in fact *reify and justify* the existing hierarchies and divisions of society. We can then understand why it is that so much of recent literary and cultural critique is suspicious of theories of universal or essential human nature. By seeing great works of art as simply celebrating a universal human nature and working with transhistorical and transcultural ideas of humanity we in fact disguise their powerful critiques of injustice and inequality.

Finally, I want to suggest, the history of racial thought alerts us against simple oppositions between 'science' and 'literature' and between 'nature' and 'culture'. Imperialist science divided humankind into supposedly biologically distinct species but also suggested transhistorical notions of female, male and human nature – hence, for example, all women could be seen as potentially hysterical, and at the same time white and black women were regarded as having distinct sexualities. These generalizations and divisions were also sustained by much of the literature produced in the West, although of course neither all scientists nor all writers were complicit with these visions of humankind. As has been argued by Nancy Leys Stepan, many of the scientific theories of race and gender were established by means of a *literary* and rhetorical, rather than scientific, device – that of analogy. Comparisons between blacks and women, which were not scientific at all, but anchored in commonsensical assumptions about blackness and femininity, became part of scientific language and were employed in order to establish scientific 'truths' about each of them.[18]

While the pseudo-biological understanding of racial difference certainly made it extremely pernicious, Etienne Balibar reminds us that 'biological or genetic naturalism is not the only means of naturalizing human beings and social affinities' and that 'culture can also function like a nature'.[19] Balibar makes these remarks while analysing the rise of 'neo-racism' in Europe, which he describes as a 'racism without race'. Neo-racism today is increasingly directed at (largely Muslim) immigrants into Europe and 'does not have the pseudo-biological concept of race as its main driving force'. It 'carries with it an image of Islam as a "conception of the world" which is incompatible with Europeanness'.[20] Thus Muslims are regarded as people who can never successfully assimilate into Western societies, or who are conditioned to be violent, as in much of the media coverage of Islam after the attacks on the World Trade Center and the Pentagon in the United States on 11 September 2001. Such views of race are not entirely new, nor have they risen only with the decline of pseudo-biological racism. Balibar himself connects neo-racism to the anti-Semitism of the Renaissance. More recently, Lisa Lampert indicates the congruence between Samuel Huntington's rhetoric of the 'clash of civilizations' and medieval anti-Semitism and Islamophobia.[21] As I have argued elsewhere, early modern views of Muslims and Jews are also important in reminding us that 'culture' and 'biology' have in fact never been neatly separable categories.

In our so-called postcolonial age, it is not true that colonial stereotypes about human difference or human nature have simply vanished. Nor is it true that pseudo-biological explanations for human difference have simply given way to a more culture-based notion of human diversity. In fact, we are currently witnessing a backlash of sorts, a resurgence whereby all kinds of social differences are seen to have a basis in genetics. For example, a recent study published by the journal *Genome Research* argues that 'the upper castes [in India] have a higher affinity to Europeans than to Asians, and the upper castes are significantly more similar to Europeans than are the lower castes'.[22] Colonial anthropology (using the work of people such as the imperial census commissioner, Sir Herbert Risley) had indicated precisely this division, using methods such as the infamous 'nasal index' to pronounce that the upper castes were 'Indo-Aryans' while the rest were a different race called the 'Dravidians'. Ironically, the findings of the *Genome Research* study and colonial anthropologists could be cited in support of recent efforts by organizations of Dalits, or the oppressed castes, to have caste discrimination discussed at the 2001 United Nations Conference Against Racism. The Government of India, then run by right-wing Hindu nationalists, tried to block such efforts. The well-known social anthropologist André Béteille backed the government, arguing that caste and race were dissimilar. Anthropologists, he claimed, had

> established conclusively . . . the distinction between race which is a biological category with physical markers and social groupings based on language, religion, nationality, style of life or status . . . If discrimination against disadvantaged castes can be defined as a form of racial discrimination . . . Muslims and other religious minorities will claim that they too, and not just backward castes, are victims of racial discrimination . . . The U.N. initiative will open up a Pandora's box of allegations of racial discrimination throughout the world.[23]

In this case, the cultural understanding of caste difference was cited to *prevent* social action. Dalit organizations on the other hand reiterated that caste oppression is based on ideologies of descent, and that Dalits have in effect been treated as a different species from the upper castes, not only barred from intermarrying, but also from eating, praying, studying or working with them. Does social justice depend upon caste being understood as a biological category? We are back to the point at which I began, which was considering why gay activists might entertain the idea of a gene for homosexuality. But in this case Dalit activists were not claiming that caste does have a genetic basis but observing that dominant ideologies of caste work *as if* it does.

Today we are witnessing a ferocious expansion of what Lewontin has called 'genomania' whereby genetic explanations are offered for all kinds of human behaviour and human relationships. But what is striking is how much of the new genetic 'findings' simply reiterate dominant assumptions about men, women, blacks and so forth. When someone tells us that the latest genetic research has confirmed that women are more emotional than men, or that rich white men are genetically programmed to be promiscuous, we aren't in the realm of dispassionate observation. When we are told that capitalism and aggression are both intrinsic to human nature and therefore making war and money are part of the universal and natural development of human beings, what we are seeing is genetic science and cultural values working together to intensify social difference. 'Human nature' can become a way of not just clarifying but intensifying social difference. If we indeed want to search for what is common to all humanity, we cannot do it by the simple-minded deployment of this vocabulary or by ignoring what work it does in the world around us.

Notes

1. Antonio Gramsci, *Further Selections from the Prison Notebooks*, ed. and trans. Derek Boothman (Minneapolis: University of Minnesota Press, 1995), p. 285. I would like to thank Mara Mills for this quotation and for so generously sharing her ideas with me. Also Matti Bunzl, Niranjan Karnik, Adam Sutcliff and Suvir Kaul for conversations and arguments on the subject.

2. Richard C. Lewontin, 'Should People Believe What Scientists Say? The Problem of Elite Knowledge in a Democratic Society', Penn Humanities Forum, University of Pennsylvania, 14 April 2004.

3. Alan Sinfield, *Cultural Politics, Queer Reading* (Philadelphia: University of Pennsylvania Press, and London: Routledge, 1994).

4. Larry Summers was speaking at a conference at the National Bureau of Economic Research, a non-profit economic research organization in Cambridge on 14 January 2005. Sara Rimer, 'At Harvard, The Bigger Concern of the Faculty is the President's Management Style' (the *New York Times*, 26 January 2005) suggests that Steven Pinker's views 'provided much of the foundation' for Summers' remarks about women.

5. Jonathan Marks, *What It Means To Be 98% Chimpanzee: Apes, People, and Their Genes* (Berkeley, Los Angeles and London: University of California Press, 2002), p. 87. I am indebted to this book throughout this essay.

6. The *New York Times*, 20 April 2004, Section F5.

7. Geoffrey C. Bowker and Susan Leigh Star, *Sorting Things Out: Classification and Its Consequences* (London and Cambridge, MA: MIT Press, 1999), pp. 1, 319.

8. Irad Malkin, 'Postcolonial Concepts and Ancient Greek Colonization', *Modern Language Quarterly*, 65 (2004), pp. 341–64; 345.

9. Mary Louise Pratt, *Imperial Eyes: Travel Writing and Transculturation* (London and New York: Routledge, 1992). See also Ania Loomba, *Colonialism/Postcolonialism* (London: Routledge, 1998).

10. Marks, *What It Means*, pp. 168–9.

11. Marks, *What It Means*, p. 171.

12. Quoted by Marks, *What It Means*, p. 171.

13. Edward Topsell, *The Historie of Four-Footed Beastes* (London, 1607), pp. 4, 13. See Ania Loomba, *Shakespeare, Race and Colonialism* (Oxford: Oxford University Press, 2002) for a detailed discussion of race in the early modern period.

14. Sir Thomas Herbert, *A relation of some yeares travaile, begunne anno 1626* (London, 1634), p. 17.

15. Michel de Montaigne, *The Complete Essays of Montaigne*, trans. Donald M. Frame (Stanford, CA: Stanford University Press, 1989), pp. 153, 156.

16. William Shakespeare, *The Tempest*, 2.1.141–62. All quotations from Shakespeare are taken from the *Complete Works of William Shakespeare*, ed. Stanley Wells and Gary Taylor (Oxford: Oxford University Press,

1986). All further line numbers are included in parenthesis after the quotations.

17. See Loomba, *Shakespeare, Race and Colonialism* for a fuller discussion of early modern race and *Othello*.

18. Nancy Leys Stepan, 'Race and Gender: The Role of Analogy in Science', in D. T Goldberg (ed.), *The Anatomy of Racism* (Minneapolis and London: University of Minnesota Press, 1990).

19. Etienne Balibar, 'Is There a Neo-racism?', in Etienne Balibar and Emmanuel Wallerstein, *Race, Nation, Class: Ambiguous Identities* (London: Verso, 1991), pp. 17–28; 22.

20. Balibar, 'Neo-racism', pp. 22, 24.

21. Lisa Lampert, 'Race, Periodicity, and the (Neo-) Middle Ages', *Modern Language Quarterly*, 65 (2004), pp. 391–422.

22. Michael Bamshad *et al.*, 'Genetic Evidence on the Origins of Indian Caste Populations', *Genome Research*, 11 (2001), pp. 991, 994–1004.

23. André Béteille, 'Race and Caste', *The Hindu*, 10 March 2001. Accessed at http://wcar.alrc.net/mainfile.php/For+the+negative/14/ on 25 November 2004.

9   What science can and cannot tell us about human nature

Kenan Malik

Few people would deny that humans are animals, evolved beings with evolved bodies and evolved minds. Equally, few would deny that humans are in some fashion distinct from other animals. In part, at least, the debate about what science can or cannot tell us about human nature is a debate about how we should understand the relationship between continuity and distinctiveness, and about whether we can explain what is distinctive about humans in the same terms as we explain the continuity of humans with the rest of the natural world. In recent decades there has been a conceptual shift in the way we approach these two questions. We can see an increasing tendency to deny the exceptional character of being human and to view humans as little more than sophisticated animals – in other words to stress the continuities at the expense of the discontinuities. Driving this shift have been both scientific and political arguments. Let me deal with the scientific arguments first; I will return to the political issues later.

For many natural scientists, any acknowledgement of human exceptionalism smacks of mysticism. The primatologist Frans de Waal, for instance, suggests that the traditional distinction between nature and culture is one more expression of 'outdated Western dualism'. Natural selection, he argues, 'has produced our species, including our cultural abilities. Culture is part of human nature.'[1] And since human nature can be understood through 'a combination of neurophysiology and deep genetic history', as E. O. Wilson has put it, so all that appears distinctive about human beings – language, morality, reason, culture itself – is not in fact that exceptional, and can be understood in the same way as can any natural phenomenon.

The naturalistic viewpoint, the biological anthropologist Rob Foley suggests, 'turns every large philosophical and metaphysical question into what are often straightforward and even boring technical ones'. For example, Darwinism turns the question 'Where do humans come from?' into a specific discussion about the time and the place where humans evolved. Similarly, Darwinists deal with the question 'What is unique about humans?' by comparing human anatomy, physiology and behaviour with that of non-human animals. 'Human origins and ultimately human nature', Foley insists, 'are not philosophical questions.'[2]

Yet Foley himself concedes that matters are not so simple. Darwinists cannot simply ignore wider philosophical issues when they consider human evolution. For instance, Foley observes that 'the question "When did we become human?". . . may appear a straightforward question about the fossil record'. In practice, however, the answer 'turns out to hinge not just on the technicalities of dating fossils, but on the criteria by which humanity is defined . . . Is it language, culture, bipedalism, intelligence, tool-making, or any other number of characteristics?'[3] And, as even a cursory glance at the history of debates about human evolution reveals, these criteria are often shaped by wider social influences.

There is, I think, a more profound problem, too. It is not simply that the data of science require an interpretative framework. The very character of natural science, I believe, constrains what it can tell us about what it is to be human.

A paradox of natural science is that its success in understanding nature has created problems for its understanding of human nature. The success of science derives from the way that it has 'disenchanted' the natural world, in Max Weber's phrase. Whereas the pre-scientific world viewed the universe as full of purpose and desire, the scientific revolution transformed nature into an inert, mindless entity. At the heart of the scientific methodology is its view of nature, and of natural organisms, as machines; not because ants or apes are inanimate, or because they work like watches or TVs, but because, like all machines, they lack self-consciousness and will. Humans, however, are not disenchanted creatures. We possess – or, at least, we believe we possess – purpose and agency, self-consciousness and will, qualities that science has expunged from the rest of nature. Uniquely among organisms, human beings are both objects of nature and subjects that can, to some extent at least, shape our own fate. We are biological beings, and under the purview of biological and physical laws. But we are also reflexive, rational, social beings able consciously to exploit biological and physical laws to overcome the constraints those very same laws place upon us.

The very development of the scientific method has exacerbated this paradox of being human. To study nature scientifically requires us to make a distinction between a humanity that is a thinking subject and a nature that presents itself to thought but is itself incapable of thought. When studying 'external' nature the distinction between the thinking subject and the object of study is easy to make. But with the study of humans, such a neat division becomes impossible: human beings are simultaneously the subject that thinks and the object of that thought. We can understand humans as beings within nature that can be studied by science. But the very act of studying humans in this fashion takes them in a certain sense outside of nature because of the distinction we must make between an objective nature and a thinking humanity. This is, in Kate Soper's words, 'the paradox of humanity's simultaneous immanence and transcendence'. Nature 'is that which Humanity finds itself within, and to which in some sense it belongs, and also that from which it seems excluded in the very moment it reflects upon either its otherness or its belongingness'.[4]

Humans, in other words, have a 'dual character', as both object and subject. And this dual character necessarily shapes the debate about continuities and discontinuities between the human and non-human world. Over the centuries many thinkers have pointed to some specific quality – culture, reason, tool-use, language, morality – as that which makes humans distinct. Others, especially in the wake of Darwin, have argued that each of these qualities can also be found in non-human animals: that many animals use tools, act according to reason, have the capacity for language, act morally and possess culture.

I don't want to enter this debate. But I do want to suggest that the meaning of all these qualities is different for humans than it is for non-humans, because only humans exist as subjects. Take, for instance, culture. Frans de Waal defines culture as 'knowledge and habits [that] are acquired from others'. It explains why 'two groups of the same species may behave differently'.[5] Under this definition many species of animals can be viewed as cultured. Chimpanzees, for instance, possess some 39 cultural habits. One group has learnt to use a stick to hunt for termites, another to deploy two stones as 'hammer' and 'anvil' to open notoriously hard palm-nuts. Each habit is peculiar to that group; an individual chimp learns by imitating others within the group.[6]

Humans, however, do not simply acquire habits from others. We also constantly innovate, transforming ourselves, individually and collectively, as we do so. There is a fundamental difference between a process by which certain chimpanzees have learnt to use two stones to crack open a palm-nut and a process through which humans have engineered the industrial revolution, unravelled the secrets of their own genome and developed the concept of universal rights.

Many animals may well be cultural creatures under de Waal's definition. But humans are entirely different kinds of cultural beings. In the seven million years or so since the evolutionary lines of humans and chimpanzees first diverged on either side of Africa's Great Rift Valley, chimpanzees have evolved, but, in comparative terms, their behaviour and lifestyles have barely changed. Human behaviour and lifestyles have clearly been transformed out of all recognition. Humans have learnt to learn from previous generations, to improve upon their work, and to establish a momentum to human life and culture that has taken us from cave art to quantum physics and the conquest of space. All animals have an evolutionary past. Only humans make history.

Science has expunged self-consciousness, purposiveness and agency from the natural world. But self-consciousness, purposiveness and agency remain crucial aspects of the human world. How, then, can natural science explain what it is to be human?

One approach has been to argue that self-consciousness, purposiveness and agency are illusions, phenomena that natural selection has designed us to believe in, not because they are true, but because they are useful. As the neuroscientist Colin Blakemore has put it, when 'we feel ourselves to be in control of an action, that feeling itself is the product of our brain, whose machinery has been designed, on the basis of its functional utility, by means of natural selection'. According to Blakemore, 'To choose a spouse, a job, a religious creed – or even to choose to rob a bank – is the peak of a causal chain that runs back to the origin of life and down to the nature of atoms and molecules.'[7]

We think we are in charge, but in reality there is no self that can take charge. There is simply the machinery of the brain churning away, thanks to a chain of causal links that goes back to the Big Bang itself. A variation on this argument is provided by the psychologist Susan Blakemore, who adopts Richard Dawkins' notion of a *meme*, a unit of culture that inhabits, or rather *parasitises*, our brains. Blakemore suggests that 'Instead of thinking of our ideas as our own creations, and working for us, we have to think of them as autonomous selfish memes, working only to get themselves copied.' Since 'we cannot find either beliefs or the self that believes' by looking into somebody's head, she argues, so we must conclude that there are no such things as beliefs or selves, 'only a person arguing, a brain processing the information, memes being copied or not'.[8]

The trouble with arguments such as these is that, by their own criteria, they provide us with no reason for believing in them. From an evolutionary point of view, truth is contingent. Darwinian processes are driven by the need, not to ascertain truth, but to survive and reproduce. Of course, survival often requires organisms to have correct facts about the world. A zebra that believed that lions were friendly, or a chimpanzee that enjoyed the stench of rotting food, would not survive for long. But although natural selection often ensures that an organism possesses the correct facts, it does not always do so. Indeed, the argument that self-consciousness and agency are illusions designed by natural selection relies on the idea that evolution can select for untruths about the world because such untruths aid survival.

If, then, our cognitive capacities were simply evolved dispositions, there would be no way of knowing which of these capacities lead to true beliefs and which to false ones. Even defenders of the naturalistic hypothesis recognize this problem. The late Robert Nozick, for instance, suggested that 'Reason tells us about reality because reality shapes reason, selecting for what seems "evident".' But, he acknowledged, if this is the case, then the evolutionary explanation of reason itself may be suspect:

> The evolutionary explanation itself is something we arrive at, in part by the use of reason to support evolutionary theory in general and also this particular application of it. Hence it does not provide a reason-independent justification of reason, and although it grounds reason in facts independent of reason, this grounding is not accepted by us independently of reason.[9]

Evolutionary theory provides an explanation of, but not a justification for, reason. Although it grounds reason in certain evolutionary facts, this is causal grounding only. These facts are not supposed to provide us with grounds for accepting the validity or reliability of reason. But, as the philosopher Thomas Nagel points out, without a justification for reason, we have no basis on which to accept the evolutionary hypothesis as an explanation for it:

> Unless it is coupled with an independent basis for confidence in reason, the evolutionary hypothesis is threatening rather than reassuring . . . I have to be able to believe that the evolutionary explanation is consistent with the proposition that I follow the rules of logic because they are correct – not merely because I am biologically programmed to do so. But to believe that, I have to be justified independently in believing that they are correct. And this cannot be merely on the basis of my contingent psychological disposition, together with the hypothesis that it is the product of natural selection.[10]

What this means, Nagel points out, is that 'the evolutionary hypothesis is acceptable only if reason does not need its support. One cannot embed all one's reasoning in a psychological theory, including the reasonings that have led to that psychological theory.'[11] The epistemological buck, as Nagel puts it, must stop somewhere.

The logic of the kind of argument put forward by Colin Blakemore and Susan Blackmore, in other words, undermines our confidence in its own veracity. For, if we are simply sophisticated animals or machines, then we cannot have any confidence in the claim that we are only sophisticated animals or machines. We are only able to do science because we possess the capacity to transcend our evolutionary heritage, because we exist as subjects, rather than simply as objects. The relationship between humans as physically determined beings, and humans as conscious agents – between humans as objects and humans as subjects – is clearly one of the most difficult problems for scientists and philosophers. While analytically we can talk of humans either as subjects or as objects, in reality humans are simultaneously both subject and object. We have at present no conceptual framework within which to consider such an ontological peculiarity. But denying one or other aspects of our humanness is not a way of solving the conundrum.

Another way of putting this is that human nature is not simply natural. We often lose sight of this because of the ambiguity of the concept of human nature. On the one hand, human nature means that which expresses the essence of being human, what Darwinists call 'species-typical' behaviour. On the other, it means that which is constituted by nature; in Darwinian terms, that which is the product of natural selection.

In non-human animals the two meanings are synonymous. What dogs and bats or sharks typically do as a species, they do because of natural selection. But this is not necessarily true of humans. There are certainly species-typical human behaviours and social forms designed through natural selection. But humans, unlike non-human animals, can also forge universal values and behaviours through social interaction and historical progress. In this sense the human essence – what we consider to be the common properties of our humanity – is as much a product of our historical and cultural development as it is of our biological heritage. The fact that humans are rational, social beings places certain constraints and creates certain opportunities that can shape the ways in which we think about the world and organize our collective lives. Being rational we are able to apprehend the regularities of the objective world and to draw conclusions from them. Being social creates certain opportunities common to all societies – the possibility of a division of labour, for instance – and imposes certain universal restrictions, such as the need for social order. Being both social and rational means that the common social goals, opportunities and constraints are often tackled in a similar fashion in different societies.

A good illustration of the way that human universals can be the product of social, not biological, development, comes in an example that is often cited as evidence for the view that all universals are evolved traits. Over the past three decades a number of anthropologists have shown that many pre-industrial societies have developed taxonomies of the natural world that are remarkably consistent with the modern Linnaean system. The anthropologist Brent Berlin, who pioneered the cross-cultural society of biological classification, suggests that there exists a 'default' taxonomy characteristic of all traditional, or folk, societies. All such societies can recognize hundreds of species – far more than they eat or utilize in other ways – that they classify according to a complex hierarchical system. All regard the rank of species as the most important in the hierarchy, and there is a remarkably high correspondence between what such societies regard as species and what modern biologists do. All this has led some anthropologists to suggest that humans possess a special mental faculty whose job it is to distinguish between animate and inanimate objects and to classify animate ones. The rules by which people classify the living world are common to all cultures because they are hardwired into our brains.[12]

It is possible, however, to understand the universality of such taxonomic rules in a different way. All humans habitually classify all manner of things from books to weather systems. All pre-industrial societies require a good grasp of relations within the natural world. And while the flora and fauna of, say, Europe and Australia may differ, the relationships between classes of organisms remain the same the world over. The objective world, in other words, is a constant. Given all this, it is likely that many different societies are both driven to classify the natural world, and compelled to establish similar kinds of rules about the manner in which the natural world is parcelled up.

There is another way of putting this. If the capacity for biological classification is an evolved trait, it could only have arisen because the brains of some of our ancestors noticed regularities in the living world. Such people may have been better at finding food or avoiding predators; they would have survived and reproduced better than those who did not notice the regularities, and hence the trait would have spread through the population.

But here's the catch. If there exists enough regularity in the living world, and sufficient selection pressure, for nature to design a brain module that can classify the living world, then there also exists sufficient regularity and pressure for humans to create such a taxonomy-maker empirically. If nature can do it without foresight, so can humans with a little forethought. If, on the other hand, there is insufficient environmental structure or external pressure for humans to generate this taxonomy empirically, then neither is there likely to be sufficient structure or pressure for it to evolve naturally.[13]

I do not know – and nor does anyone else – whether the apparently universal capacity to classify the natural world along similar lines is an evolved trait or not. All I'm suggesting is that for humans, unlike for non-human animals, such universals can arise without the help of nature because humans are rational, social beings.

In 1945 the anthropologist George Murdock set out a group of items which he believed occurred in 'every culture known to history or ethnography'. More recently Donald Brown has updated this with a considerably more comprehensive list.[14] These lists of universals have become celebrated and are often cited by sociobiologists and evolutionary psychologists making the case for the evolved character of human psychology.[15] What is striking about both lists is the manner in which they conflate distinct categories of human activity under the single rubric of 'human nature'. Donald Brown's list of universals, for instance, includes examples of psychological traits (emotions, empathy, sexual attraction, mental maps); individual behaviour (baby-talk, crying, dreaming, thumb-sucking, tickling); cultural beliefs (the classification of body parts, the imposition of taboos on certain foods, belief in the cyclical nature of time); social mores (childcare, feasting, the giving of gifts, sanctions for crimes); economic structures (a division of labour, cooperative labour);

intellectual, artistic and symbolic endeavours (melody, music, rhythm, symbolism, imagery, myths); and technological achievements (the use of fire, the making of tools, the creation of medicines, the building of shelters).

Such categorical conflation reflects the ambiguity in the concept of human nature that I have already mentioned. For what is also striking about these lists is how many of these universals can be understood in social or cultural terms, rather than necessarily as evolved adaptations. The apparent universal classification of weather conditions, for instance, relies on objective regularities in the world, the capacity of humans to apprehend such regularities and the social need for humans to understand such regularities. Creation of regimes of cleanliness is crucial given that humans live in communities, fear the spread of disease and have the rational capacity to design ways of avoiding this. The practice of using personal names becomes important in a species in which individuals not only have distinct characters but distinct duties and responsibilities for which they can be held to account. And so on. In each case, the criteria for the development of these traits are social needs and opportunities that are universal. In other words, the universal existence of these needs and opportunities within human communities means that it is quite possible for every human culture to have developed such traits (or to have appropriated them from other cultures) without these necessarily having been designed by natural selection.

A second expression of the historicity of the human essence lies in the way that human nature is often normative. Salman Rushdie has suggested that if human nature did not exist, then 'the idea of universals – human rights, moral principles, international law – would have no legitimacy'.[16] This idea has become central to the contemporary science of human nature. A number of evolutionary psychologists have suggested, for instance, that revulsion at the practice of slavery is part of human nature because we have a natural aversion to being humiliated and imprisoned. Francis Fukuyama has taken this argument to show that liberal capitalism lies at the end of history because its beliefs and institutions 'are grounded in assumptions about human nature that are far more realistic than those of their competitors'.[17]

Certainly, our *capacity* for moral thought is most likely an evolved trait. But this is not the same as saying that *values* are natural. Take the question of slavery and the idea of equal human worth. For most of human history slavery was regarded as natural as individual freedom is today. Only in the past 200 years have we begun to view the practice with revulsion. We have done so partly because of the political ideas generated by the Enlightenment, partly because of the changing economic needs of capitalism, and partly because of the social struggles of the enslaved and the oppressed. Certainly, today we view opposition to slavery as an essential aspect of our humanity, and see those who advocate slavery as in some way *inhuman* – but that's a belief we have arrived at historically, not naturally. To understand human values such as the belief in equality we need to explore not so much human psychology as human history.

A final illustration of the historicity of the human essence lies, paradoxically, in the universality of great art. Many thinkers from George Steiner to E. O. Wilson have suggested that great artists such as Dante, Shakespeare or Beethoven are appreciated across cultures and over time because their work taps into the universal features of human nature. In his book *The Blank Slate*, Steven Pinker argues that art is 'in our genes', because nature endows us with an innate aesthetic sense. Hence Shakespeare is appreciated in twenty-first-century Japan as much as he was in seventeenth-century England. Modernism, on the other hand, has been an aesthetic failure, Pinker suggests, because it developed out of what he calls its 'militant denial of human nature'.[18]

I don't want to enter here into a discussion about the merits or otherwise of modernism, but I do want to suggest that Pinker misunderstands the nature of Shakespeare's genius. Shakespeare did not simply articulate universal themes of love, lust and power; he also helped fashion a new vision of what it is to be human. Shakespeare's characters speak to us in a different way because, unlike previous literary figures, they possess a self-consciousness as we possess self-consciousness. As the American critic Harold Bloom puts it, 'Insofar as we ourselves value, and deplore, our own personalities, we are the heirs of Falstaff and Hamlet, and of all the persons who throng Shakespeare's theater of what might be called the colors of the spirit.'[19]

Shakespeare was not alone in developing a new language through which to understand our emotions and feelings. The kind of sensibility that Shakespeare brought to the stage, his near-contemporaries Rembrandt and Vermeer worked into a canvas. Rembrandt is regarded as the first, perhaps the greatest, of all self-portraitists because when we view his paintings we come face to face, for the first time in history, with a person, a self. It is impossible to look at his self-portraits, especially of old age, and not see Rembrandt himself. In a similar way, Vermeer's paintings reveal the new eyes through which painters now viewed their subjects as *persons*.

What we are witnessing in Shakespeare, Rembrandt, Vermeer, and countless others, are the beginnings of the modern idea of subjectivity, of the individual as a rational agent, and of the marking out of the private sphere as we conceive of it today. It was in this period that the idea of the 'inner man' began to take shape, an idea that, most importantly, was given philosophical shape through Descartes' concept of the thinking subject. When Descartes suggested that *cogito ergo sum* he was helping to create the idea of 'I' in a modern sense.

The motor for these changes in self-conception lay in particular social and economic developments in early modern Europe – the spread of market relations, the creation of a merchant class, the belief that wealth and privilege was the product of an individual's activities, not simply a divine gift or the result of one's social status. The consequence was to establish a notion of self and of personality that today we take to be natural because we cannot imagine any other way of thinking about such concepts.

Human emotions are the product of our evolutionary heritage. But the self that possesses those emotions has been forged in the furnace of history. That's why Shakespeare's work is paradoxically both universal and contingent. It is universal because today, whether we live in Britain or in Japan, we are able to recognize in his characters the workings of our own self. It is contingent because this concept of the self was not given by nature but made in history. Human nature, then, cannot simply be understood as a natural phenomenon, because it is also historically constituted. And this historicity of human nature establishes limits to naturalistic explanations of what it is to be human.

Someone might say, 'Hold on, does not a scientific view of the world require a naturalistic philosophy? In questioning naturalism, are we not in danger of invoking supernatural or divine explanations of how the world operates, opening the way to, say, Creationism and the like?' The answer to this depends upon the definition of naturalism, or rather upon the redefinition that has taken place in recent decades. Originally, as the concept developed through the seventeenth and eighteenth centuries, 'naturalism' meant the ability to explain all events and phenomena without recourse to the supernatural and the divine. It came to be understood as a liberation from the dogmas of religion and the conservative social order for which they served as an ideology, as well as a declaration of independence for scientific inquiry into both the nature of the world and human nature. In this sense I am a fully-fledged, card-carrying naturalist.

In recent decades, though, there has been a redefinition of naturalism, which is now widely taken to mean not simply the rejection of supernatural accounts but also the acceptance of the idea that the explanations of natural science suffice to explain all phenomena, not just the phenomena of nature; in other words that mental and social phenomena can be reduced to the physical. Naturalism has been reformulated as an all-embracing physicalism. For a contemporary naturalist the only conceptual system in terms of which the world and its processes can be reliably characterized is that of the physical sciences of nature. In contemporary naturalism, as Frederick Olafson has put it, 'The world and nature are one and the same, and everything in them is of the same ontological type.'[20] Thus Edward O. Wilson suggests that 'sociology and other social sciences, as well as the humanities, are the last branches of biology'.[21] And Richard Dawkins believes that 'Science is the only way to understand the real world.'[22]

It's a view, I believe, that confuses the physical world with the 'real' world. For, as Mary Midgley has pointed out, 'Toothache is as real as teeth' and 'debt is as real as the house that was bought with it'.[23] The social and the mental are as real as the physical. But the social and the mental cannot be understood simply in physical terms. I am not suggesting that consciousness and agency are beyond rational explanation, but rather that they cannot be *fully* explained by the precepts of *natural* science because a physical description of the human being does not provide a *sufficient* explanation for such phenomena.

The irony of contemporary physicalism is that, while its starting point is a rejection of Cartesian dualism, its inability to make sense of agency leads it back into the Cartesian swamp. Richard Dawkins has rightly suggested that human values are not rooted in nature but are non-natural creations. 'We are built as gene machines', he wrote in *The Selfish Gene*, but we also possess 'the power to turn against our creators'. Humans, 'alone on earth', Dawkins suggests, 'can rebel against the tyranny of the selfish replicators'.[24] But whence comes our power 'to turn against our creators' and to rebel against their selfishness if we are built simply as 'gene machines'? Human values, presumably, do not float down from the sky, but emerge out of human thought and behaviour. How then do they originate if not through 'natural selection and neurophysiology' that contemporary naturalists hold to be the basis of all other behaviours? Steven Pinker explains it like this: 'The mechanistic stance allows us to understand what makes us tick and how we fit into the physical universe. When those discussions wind down for the day, we go back to talking about each other as free and dignified human beings.'[25] But freedom and dignity seem here to have no relationship to the physical world, and hence to human nature. They seem to float free in a universe of their own. We have jumped headlong, in other words, back into the Cartesian swamp where the physical is unconnected to the moral world. As Frans de Waal has said of such arguments, 'These authors want to have it both ways: human behaviour is an evolutionary product except when it is hard to explain.' What is lacking in such arguments, de Waal points out, 'is an indication of how we can possibly negate our genes'.[26]

De Waal's own solution is to see morality as natural, in the same way as is culture. The trouble with this argument, however, is the same as in the debate over culture: it ignores the dual character of being human. Morality in human life is based on our existence as subjects – that is, as moral agents capable of taking responsibility for our actions and who, through history, have developed our moral sensibilities. What we might call morality in the non-human world describes behaviours by beings that are objects – beings that do not possess agency, cannot take responsibility, and for whom the notion of moral progress is inapplicable. Once you fail to make such a distinction then you are forced to accept, as Colin Blakemore does, that moral responsibility has no real meaning but is a fiction we've created, because otherwise society could not work.[27] If, on the other hand, one believes that moral responsibility and political agency are more than fictions, then one has to take seriously the existence of humans as subjects.

The distinction I am drawing is between a *mechanistic*, a *mysterian* and a *materialist* view of the world. A mechanistic view sees human beings largely as objects through which nature acts. A mysterian view suggests that there are aspects of human existence not knowable to mere mortals. A materialist view, on the other hand, understands human beings without resort to mystical explanations. But it also sees humans as exceptional because humans, unlike any other beings, possess consciousness and agency. And understanding human consciousness and agency requires us to understand humans not just as natural, but also as historical and social beings.

But it's just this view of humans as social and historical beings – as creatures who can transform themselves and the world around them – that today is in such bad odour. As the philosopher John Gray puts it in his book *Straw Dogs*, 'Those who struggle to change the world' are merely seeking 'consolation for a truth they are too weak to bear'. Their 'faith that the world can be transformed by human will is a denial of their own mortality'. Like all animals, we're all going to die, seems to be the argument, so why bother with grand schemes of social change? Gray rejects the idea that human consciousness and agency have any value, or indeed are any more than absurd illusions. 'The freest human being', he suggests, 'is not one who acts on reasons he has chosen for himself, but one who never has to choose. Such a human being has the perfect freedom of a wild animal – or a machine.'[28]

We live in a time that is deeply pessimistic about the human condition. A century of unparalleled bloodshed and destruction has created a widespread scepticism about human capacities. For many people, human activity and human reason are themselves the sources of most of the ills of the world. Half a millennium ago, Descartes viewed reason as 'the noblest thing we can have because it makes us in a certain way equal to God and exempts us from being his subjects'. Today, many view human reason as a tool for destruction rather than betterment. As the biologist David Ehrenfeld put it in his emblematically titled book *The Arrogance of Humanism*, what he objects to is 'a supreme faith in human reason – its ability to confront and solve the many problems that humans face, its ability to rearrange both the world of Nature and the affairs of men and women so that human life will prosper'.[29]

There is a widespread feeling that every impression that humans make upon the world is for the worse. The attempt to master nature appears to have led to global warming and species depletion. The attempt to master society, many feel, led directly to Auschwitz and the gulags. We no longer believe, Michael Ignatieff has observed, that 'material progress entails or enables moral progress'. We eat well, we drink well, we live well 'but we do not have good dreams'. The Holocaust 'remains a ghost at our feast'.[30] 'In a real sense', notes the ecologist Murray Bookchin, 'we seem to be afraid of ourselves – of our uniquely human attributes. We seem to be suffering from a decline in human self-confidence and in our ability to create ethically meaningful lives that enrich humanity and the non-human world.'[31]

As we have become more pessimistic about the human condition, as the exceptional status of human beings has seemed at best mere self-delusion, at worst dangerously hubristic, so the idea that humans are just beasts (literally and metaphorically) has appeared both scientifically plausible and culturally acceptable. The history of the twentieth century, Rob Foley argues, has transformed our vision of humanity, leading to 'a loss of confidence in the extent to which humans could be said to be on a pedestal above the swamp of animal brutishness': 'The camps of Dachau and Belsen, the millions killed in religious wars, the extent of poverty, famine and disease, and the almost boundless capacity of humans to do damage to each other at national and personal levels have, in the twentieth century, rather dented human self-esteem.'[32] The Victorians believed that humans were closer to the angels than to the apes. During the course of the twentieth century, however, Foley notes, 'apes have become more angelic' while humans have become 'more apish'. 'Where it was originally thought that humans were the advanced and progressive form of life and other animals the more primitive', he concludes, 'now it may be argued that the animal within us is our noble side, and humanity or civilization the blacker side – a complete reversal of the original Victorian image.'[33]

The pessimism of contemporary culture, in other words, has cleared a space for a new vision that seeks to deny the exceptional qualities of being human. This retreat from humanism, and the rejection of human exceptionalism, makes, I believe, for both bad science and bad politics. It makes for bad science because it is a view of humanness that ignores an essential quality of our being – agency. Trying to explain away agency is not the same as providing a rational explanation for its existence. And it makes for bad politics because once we accept that human agency – and human reason – are forces for destruction rather than betterment, then we lose the only means we possess for human advancement, whether social, moral or technological.

The tension between scientific naturalism and human exceptionalism remains unresolved. It seems crucial to think of humans as conscious agents capable of rational thought and collective action if science itself is to advance. Yet by making humans into conscious agents we seem to separate them off from the rest of nature, and hence suggest that the language of natural science cannot fully encompass our humanness. Historically, though, this tension has been a highly creative one, helping to develop both a more rational humanism and a science of humanity compelled to address the exceptional character of human nature. The tension only becomes a problem when we attempt to resolve it by assuming either that we cannot understand human beings using reason, or that we can only understand humans mechanistically. We will, I believe, develop in time a conceptual framework that allows us to mediate between scientific naturalism and human exceptionalism. In the meantime, we should recognize the tension as a reflection of the dual character of being human, as both natural objects and historical subjects.

Notes

1. Frans de Waal, *The Ape and the Sushi Master: Cultural Reflections of a Primatologist* (London: Allen Lane, 2001), p. 8.

2. Rob Foley, *Humans Before Humanity: An Evolutionary Perspective* (Oxford: Blackwell, 1995), pp. 17, 20.

3. *Humans Before Humanity*, p. 20.

4. Kate Soper, *What is Nature? Culture, Politics and the Non-human* (Oxford: Blackwell, 1995), p. 49.

5. de Waal, *The Ape and the Sushi Master*, p. 6.

6. A. Whiten, J. Goodall, W. C. McGrew, T. Nishida, V. Reynolds, Y. Sugiyama, C. E. G. Tutin, R. Wrangham and C. Boesch, 'Cultures in Chimpanzees', *Nature*, 399 (17 June 1999), pp. 682–5; an online database of chimpanzee cultures can be found at http://138.251.146.69/cultures3.

7. Colin Blakemore, *The Mind Machine* (London: BBC Books, 1988), pp. 269–71.

8. Susan Blackmore, *The Meme Machine* (Oxford: Oxford University Press, 1999), p. 227.

9. Robert Nozick, *The Nature of Rationality* (Princeton, NJ: Princeton University Press, 1993), p. 112.

10. Thomas Nagel, *The Last Word* (Oxford: Oxford University Press, 1997), pp. 135–6.

11. *The Last Word*, p. 136.

12. Brent Berlin, *Ethnobiological Classification: Principles of Categorization of Plants and Animals in Traditional Societies* (Princeton, NJ: Princeton

University Press, 1992); S. Atran, 'Folk Biology and the Anthropology of Science: Cognitive Universals and Cultural Particulars', *Behavioral and Brain Sciences*, 21 (1998), pp. 547–69.

13. For more discussion of this, see Kenan Malik, *Man, Beast and Zombie: What Science Can and Cannot Tell Us About Human Nature* (London: Weidenfeld & Nicolson, 2000), pp. 252–8.

14. George P. Murdock, 'The Common Denominators of Cultures', in Ralph Linton (ed.), *The Science of Man in the World Crisis* (New York: Columbia University Press, 1945), p. 125; Donald Brown, *Human Universals* (New York: McGraw-Hill, 1991).

15. See, for instance, Edward O. Wilson, *On Human Nature* (Cambridge, MA: Harvard University Press, 1978); Steven Pinker, *The Blank Slate: The Modern Denial of Human Nature* (London: Allen Lane, 2002).

16. Salman Rushdie, 'USA: It's Human Nature', *Guardian*, 3 December 1998.

17. Francis Fukuyama, *Our Posthuman Future: Consequences of the Biotechnological Revolution* (London: Profile Books, 2002), p. 106.

18. Pinker, *The Blank Slate*, p. 416.

19. Harold Bloom, *Shakespeare: The Invention of the Human* (London: Fourth Estate, 1998), p. 4.

20. Frederick Olafson, *Naturalism and the Human Condition: Against Scientism* (London: Routledge, 2001), p. 6.

21. Edward O. Wilson, *Sociobiology: The Abridged Version* (Cambridge, MA: Belknap Press, 1975), p. 4.

22. Richard Dawkins, 'Thoughts for the Millennium', *Microsoft Encarta Encyclopaedia 2000*.

23. Mary Midgley, *Science and Poetry* (London: Routledge, 2001), p. 141.

24. Richard Dawkins, *The Selfish Gene* (1975), 2nd edn (Oxford: Oxford University Press, 1989), p. 201.

25. *The Selfish Gene*, p. 56.

26. de Waal, *The Ape and the Sushi Master*, p. 347.

27. Interview in 'Cells, Souls and Science', BBC Radio 4, 18 July 2002. A transcript of the text can be found at www.kenanmalik.com/tv/biotechnology.

28. John Gray, *Straw Dogs: Thoughts on Humans and Other Animals* (London: Granta, 2002), pp. 96, 114.

29. David Ehrenfeld, *The Arrogance of Humanism* (Oxford: Oxford University Press, 1981), p. 4.

30. Michael Ignatieff, 'The Ascent of Man', *Prospect* (October 1999), pp. 28–31.

31. Murray Bookchin, *Re-enchanting Humanity: A Defence of the Human Spirit Against Antihumanism, Misanthropy, Mysticism and Primitivism* (London: Cassell, 1995), p. 1.

32. Foley, *Humans Before Humanity*, p. 36.

33. *Humans Before Humanity*, p. 36.

10 The cat, the chisel, and the grave: an answer to the question 'do we need a theory of human nature in order to act?'

Philip Pullman

On the whole, I'm not at ease among theories. Though I'll qualify that at once by saying that it's other people's theories that make me uneasy; my own are entirely congenial. But theories, wherever they come from, work like photographic filters: if you're taking a picture with black and white film, and you want to bring out the whiteness of the clouds and darken the blue of the sky, a yellow filter over the lens will do it for you. A red filter will do it even more vividly, and a green filter will do something else entirely. They work by blocking out some of the information in order to clarify the rest. They don't put in things that aren't there: they make it easier to see certain things that are there.

Theories of literature work the same way. If you read *Wuthering Heights* through the filter of Marxist theory, for example, you'll see various social relationships that weren't easily visible before. If you read it through the filter of Freudianism, it will bring to the eye all kinds of Oedipal repressions and tensions involving sexual feelings; and feminist theory and postcolonialist theory will show you yet other aspects of the novel which are certainly there, but not easy to see among all the rest of the information.

The wrong inference to make from this would be to say that if we look at something without the filter of a theory we'll see it truly, or clearly, or as it really is. But that wouldn't be true. We have plenty of built-in filters that we're not always aware of, some of them the accretions of habit, some acquired in the process of our education and then forgotten about, some the result of natural selection operating on our remote ancestors, some the consequences of our own individual temperaments. The best we can do, it seems to me, is to be aware that we see everything through filters of one sort or another, and to be modest about the claims we make for this theory or that one.

However, I think it's true to say that some filters, some ways of looking at the world, are more useful than others. One of the most useful is the scientific method. I think it far more likely than not that a great deal of what science shows us is true, is really there, and I don't believe that science is only true for us, and might not be true for someone in another place or another time. So I'm inclined to listen to science with some respect.

The question I'm considering here is whether I need a theory of human nature in order to act. And since what I do is write stories, the question is: would I write better stories, or would it be easier to write the sort of stories I already write, if I had a theory-filter, a coherent set of statements about human nature, that I consciously put in place every time I began a day's work?

Because writing stories is difficult and I welcome anything, any form of superstition, even, that will help me when I sit down with a pen in my hand; and I still use a pen, because I have a lucky one. So if I thought a theory would help, I'd use it.

But I don't think it would. I think I'd feel oppressed by it. I'd feel like the representative of a point of view, a delegate, rather than a storyteller; I'd be constantly checking to find the party line, and would make sure I didn't write anything that contradicted it. It would make for a feeling of dead weight, when I needed to be most light. It would remind me of what I thought being human ought to be like, when I needed to be least human.

I'll say a little about that last statement first, because it involves the business of narration, which is fundamental to the whole process. When a novel is told in the first person, it's obvious that the narrating voice is 'made up': the voice that tells the story belongs to one of the characters invented by the novelist. But what happens when a story is told in the third person, by someone whom we can only refer to as the 'narrator'? And here I mean the sort of storytelling that began to look rather old-fashioned in the twentieth century, when modernism made it almost compulsory for fiction to be mediated to the reader through the minutely notated flickerings of consciousness in this mind or that, or through the refractions and displacements of formal experiment.

The sort of fiction I mean is the confident and unembarrassed story-telling that characterizes many of the novels of the nineteenth century. That was the sort of story I wanted to write, and in order to do so, I had to discover how to make that third-person, anonymous, 'omniscient' narrative voice work. And I was in for a surprise.

Because until then, like many young or unsophisticated readers, I'd assumed that the narrative voice was the voice of the novelist, pure and simple. But as soon as I tried to write a story in such a way, I quickly came to see that the telling voice wasn't my own, but that of some other character – an invented one just as much as those characters who have names and do things in the story – but a character of an odd and different sort. It isn't possible for a human being to look into someone else's mind and tell us what they're thinking, and then to look with equal ease into a third person's, or to look into the future and say what will happen several years hence, but the narrator can; and if you pretend that the characters you're writing about are real, with all the usual human characteristics, then you can only conclude that the narrator isn't like the rest of them, but is much stranger. In fact the narrator is the oddest, the most evasive and mysterious, the most protean character in fiction: more subtle than Hamlet, richer than Falstaff, more puzzling and contradictory even than the God of the Old Testament. The narrator is old and young, foolish and wise, male and female, sceptical and credulous, innocent and experienced, timid and brazen, transitory and immortal – all at once. The view I've come to is that this unnamed narrator is a sprite.

To write with this extraordinary voice is such a privilege that it's a mystery to me why any writer would choose to enter the narrow and ill-lit prison of the first person. But you can see why writing fiction according to a theory of human nature – or a theory of anything else – would put the sprite in a bottle, seal it with lead, and weigh it down with chains.

On the contrary, what I need when I sit down to write a story is not a theory, but images: images of ghosts, demons, spirits, hobgoblins, magic rituals, and diabolical possession; images of a glance that begins with a smile and ends in a blush; images of a garden suffused with moonlight and with a feeling of loss and happiness inextricably commingled; images of a girl trapped and hiding in a room she shouldn't have gone into, and overhearing something that will change her life; images of . . . and so on: *images that yet fresh images beget*, out of the depths of the unconscious mind, or out of the structures of the brain such as the fusiform gyrus, where (according to the neuroscientist V. S. Ramachandran) the sensory metaphors of synaesthesia, and maybe all metaphors, are generated.

So I need to examine some images. But I've found that the way to deal with such things is to creep up on them, and not switch on the lights and subject them to interrogation. You need to make them think you're not looking at them at all; you need to pretend to be looking at something else entirely. If you do that, you can see other things faintly at the edge of your vision, which flee away if you try to look at them directly. And there are three things hovering there in the semi-darkness, which I think might have a bearing on this human nature business. One is a question, another is an observation, and the third is an epitaph.

The question is this: how is it that I know when a story's going wrong? If I'm making up something new from scratch, how can there be a right way and a wrong way of doing it, a right shape and a wrong shape?

Because this sense is very clear and strong; there's no mistaking it. I can think of several origins for this feeling, and here are five of them.

It might be that there is a sort of Platonic realm of absolute perfection for every story that could ever be told, and that when I write I can experience it directly in some mysterious way, and sense when I'm getting warm or cold with regard to the 'pure' story, close to it or further away.

It might be cultural conditioning: it might be the experience of hearing and reading a lot of stories of a particular sort, and coming to think that that's the only natural way for a story to be, and feeling uncomfortable unless I'm with something familiar. In other words, what the *right shape* is could be purely arbitrary, and it's just that I'm used to that sort of shape.

It might be the faint apprehension of something that's definitely below the level of conscious perception most of the time. We've heard about experiments that show how our muscles begin to move before we consciously decide to make them. Maybe my writing hand has already decided what the story should be, and my satisfaction or unease with the way it's going is a result of either getting close to what's already been decided or going away from it. So my sense of *the right shape* and *the wrong shape* might be an awareness that what I take to be my conscious decision-making life is an illusion, and that in fact I'm determined or programmed by something below my conscious perception.

As a variation on that, I might be being guided by a higher power. I was recently told by one person, expert in her field, that I was channelling truths from the spirit world, and then by someone else, equally expert in hers, that my work clearly showed evidence of the unconscious working out of Oedipal conflicts. In neither case, apparently, was I – the conscious I – greatly responsible for it. So the feeling I'm talking about, as I say, might come from the fact that I'm being guided from somewhere else, and that occasionally there's a break in transmission.

Finally, it might be the fact that my own narrative nerves and muscles are wonderfully developed; that, like a football player who has practised and practised until he can kick a ball into the corner of the net every time, I am just good at what I do. So my sense of 'No, that's wrong' and 'Yes, that's right' are the sort of semi-automatic adjustments and reflections and calculations that any practitioner of any complex activity makes all the time, and that get better with practice.

Anyway, my sense that *something is going wrong* and, elsewhere, or later, my sense that *this is the right way to do it* could be due to any of those things. For reasons of *amour-propre* I prefer some of them to others, naturally. I also think some of them are simply more likely than others.

But if I don't know where this sense comes from, I can describe roughly what it feels like. It feels like the satisfaction we get when we hang a picture in the best place on a wall. There are places that simply look better than others. There's a sort of harmony or balance about them, and often we sense that sort of thing *before* we learn about systems of proportion such as the Golden Section. The interesting thing about learning how the Golden Section works is that it doesn't feel like something that might just as well be otherwise, such as the rules of the road. That we drive on the left is arbitrary; other countries drive just as successfully on the right. Learning about the Golden Section feels different from that: it feels like learning a truth that until now we had sensed but not clearly seen.

A similar thing happens with sound. When you learn to hear the beats that tell you that two strings are not perfectly in tune, or the harmonics that govern the intervals of a fourth, a fifth, and so on, you're not learning something arbitrary and then imposing it on otherwise unstructured or inchoate matter: you're learning how to perceive an order that already exists in nature. These things are *there*.

Well, my point about narrative is that it feels like that. Some narrative shapes are better than others. The shape of classical tragedy – great hero rises to glory before being brought low by fundamental flaw in character – is a case in point. It's a very good shape for a story. There might be a small number of these good shapes, and a much larger number of shapes that aren't so good, and you just get to know what they are. It feels like that. When you're actually doing it, it feels non-arbitrary.

But I still don't know where my sense of it comes from. However, that isn't the point. I've been sneaking up on the point while looking at something else.

This is the point: I don't know where that sense comes from, but it doesn't matter, because I *like* being in the state in which I believe all of those things at once. I don't know if that's a state of mind in which you can manipulate theories, but it's by far the best one in which to write a story. You have to learn how to be in several contradictory states of mind at the same time, not *this one for a while and then that one*, and not *this one a lot and that one just a bit*, but all of them, and many more, simultaneously, to the full, without judging between them. In fact you have to be like Schrödinger's cat, which is both alive and dead until you look at it.

So what helps me most to write stories is the ability to be in utterly contradictory states of mind, quite comfortably, at one and the same time. I should remind you that at this point I'm not talking about the narrative sprite, who is a character in the story I'm writing, but about me, writing it. Whether or not that's a theory of human nature I have no idea, but cats can do it.

That was my question. Here's my observation: you should go with the grain and not against it.

What leads me to this commonplace conclusion is the fact that I spent a lot of time and effort when I was younger trying to write stories of a kind that I wasn't good at. I tried to write the sort of thing that's called literary fiction, and I didn't do it at all well.

It wasn't until I was teaching twelve- and thirteen-year-old children, and writing plays for them to act in, that I found something I could do with freedom and exhilaration. The sort of stories I wrote for them were melodramas and fairy tales and Gothic romances. And I loved it. Eventually I made one of them into a novel, and then another, and another, and I found I was a writer of children's books, to my surprise.

But then I found myself in another corner of the same trap I'd been in before: I thought that I ought to write realism, because that was a higher order of thing than the fairy tales and the melodrama. So I wrote a couple of novels of that sort, and they're still in print, but they were nothing special.

And it was hard work – a particular kind of hard work. Not that writing novels is ever easy, but I wasn't enjoying it either. Nor do I mean that every moment of a novelist's life is a riot of happy fun; but something just wasn't right at a basic level.

I didn't realize what that was until I began to write *His Dark Materials*. Here was a story that – whether you call it fantasy or not – is at least non-everyday-realistic. And what I felt at that point was that I was coming home, that something in my nature leapt towards this way of imagining things, so that I felt a happy and confident ease when I wrote about dæmons and little people six inches high with poison spurs who ride on dragonflies. This was native to me in a way that realism, much as I'd have liked it to be, wasn't.

In fact, the way I felt was very similar to what I've felt when carving wood. The wood might be straight-grained and free from knots, the chisel might be as sharp as 20 minutes of dedicated honing can make it – but if you're going against the grain, you'll have an extra layer of difficulty to cope with. Turn the workpiece around and carve the other way, and the chisel will cut with nonchalant accuracy, and curls of smooth wood will obediently lift themselves from the surface.

It's a question of finding the grain of your own talent and going with it, not against it. You have to observe yourself closely and honestly, and see what you're good at, and what you enjoy, and what you can do with the imagination you have. Some writers are like boxwood; their talent has a tight and perfectly uniform grain that cuts as happily in one direction as another, so they can turn from history to comedy to tragedy without faltering. Others are like construction softwood, coarse-textured, incapable of taking fine carving, easily splintered. They can only do one kind of rough structure, which may be very large, strong and robust; but we're talking about carpentry and nails rather than cabinet-making and dove-tailed joints.

But whatever your talent is, you have to discover its nature and go with the grain of it. But whatever your talent is, you have to discover its nature and go with the grain of it. Life is a melancholy business otherwise: not only will you be perpetually frustrated, but the work you produce will not express the nature of what it's made of. Deal makes a good packing-case but a poor jewel-box; and if all you have to work with is costly and beautiful ebony, don't make it into joists under the floorboards where it won't be seen. The difficulty is always to discover which way the grain of your own nature runs, and that takes longer than you might think.

I said I'd end with an epitaph. You'll find this one on a tomb in the Church of St Peter Mancroft in Norwich, and whenever I go to that city I make a sentimental pilgrimage to see it. It's the tomb of a young woman. The inscription reads:

> This Stone is dedicated to the Talents and Virtues of Sophia Ann Goddard, who died 25 March 1801 aged 25. The Former shone with superior Lustre and Effect in the great School of Morals, the THEATRE, while the Latter inform'd the private Circle of Life with Sentiment, Taste, and Manners that still live in the Memory of Friendship and Affection.

I don't know any more about Sophia Goddard than her epitaph tells us, but clearly she was greatly loved and admired.

But you can see what I'm going to focus on. 'The great School of Morals, the THEATRE' – it's not easy to imagine anyone using a phrase like that today. It belongs to a particular time in the history of the theatre, and by extension in the history of fiction and narrative generally. I think of Jane Austen's famous and exactly contemporary comment about the novel in *Northanger Abbey*: that it's a work in which you find 'the most thorough knowledge of human nature, the happiest delineation of its varieties', and so on. Audiences and readers at that period saw narrative as a proper vehicle for moral enlightenment, for instruction as well as delight. The Puritans who closed the theatres down 150 years before Sophia Goddard died would have had a quite different view.

Or perhaps not all that different, after all; because both the Puritans who abhorred the immorality of the theatre, and the late eighteenth-century audiences who applauded Miss Goddard, took seriously the idea that narrative art had a true and meaningful connection with human life. They took for granted that the behaviour of human beings, in all its variety, could be depicted faithfully in stories, and that stories would have a moral effect, whether good or bad, and an emotional and intellectual effect, for that matter, on those who read them.

As a matter of fact, so do I. Together with pretty well everyone else who has ever read a book, I find that an entirely natural way of reading. As for 'nature', and what that means: I think that human nature is what we have made ourselves as well as what we were given to start with, and that culture, which includes both technology and narrative art, is the way we do the making. What we are now is partly a result of our remote ancestors' mastery of fire, for example, which meant that they could migrate into colder regions and evolve different body shapes and skin colours to cope with different climatic conditions, and adjust to different diets; and what we are now is also partly the result of enjoying, and pondering on, and emulating – or avoiding – the models of human behaviour set out for us by Homer, Shakespeare, Austen, George Eliot, Dostoevsky, etc, not to mention the great fairy tales, and passing on what wisdom we gain from it to our children.

So, finally: do you need a theory of human nature in order to write stories? I think you need a theory of your own nature. But that's not so easy to come by as you might think. You can spend years thinking that you're interested in something, only to discover eventually that you were never really interested, you just thought you should be. Self-knowledge is hard won.

And I think you need the capacity to take other people's theories very lightly indeed. Steal what you need, play with them, fool around with them, but don't whatever you do become a slave to them. Remember the cat; sometimes in order to be freely and fully human we have to be a little feline too.

Index